CW00494707

The Transparency of Things

Contemplating the
Nature of Experience

Rupert Spira

NON-DUALITY PRESS

First published November 2008 by Non-Duality Press

Typeset in Aldus 11/13
Cover design by Rupert Spira and John Gustard

Non-Duality Press, Salisbury, SP2 8JP
United Kingdom

ISBN 978-0-9558290-5-5

www.non-dualitybooks.com

This book is written with gratitude and love for Ellen, my companion, and Francis Lucille, my friend and teacher.

Contents

"*That which is, never ceases to be. That which is not,*
never comes into being."

PARMENIDES

Foreword

This book is a collection of contemplations and conversations about the nature of experience. Its only purpose, if it can be said to have any purpose at all, is to look clearly and simply at experience itself.

The conventional formulations of our experience are, in most cases, considered to be so absolutely true as to need no further investigation. Here, the opposite is the case. Absolutely nothing is taken for granted, save the conventions of language that enable us to communicate.

From an early age we are encouraged to formulate our experience in ways that seem to express and validate it, and these expressions subsequently condition the way the world appears.

'David loves Jane,' 'Tim saw the bus.' Our earliest formulations divide experience into 'I' and 'other,' 'me' and 'the world,' a subject experiencing an object. From that time on, our experience seems to validate these formulations.

However, at a certain stage it begins to dawn on us that these formulations do not *express* our experience, but rather they *condition* it.

This book does not address the particular qualities of experience itself. It explores only its fundamental nature. What is this 'I'? What is this 'other,' this 'world'? And what is this 'experiencing' that seems to join the two together?

The essential discovery of all the great spiritual traditions is the identity of Consciousness and Reality, the discovery that the fundamental nature of each one of us is identical with the fundamental nature of the universe.

This has been expressed in many different ways. 'Atman equals Brahman.' 'I and my Father are one.' 'Nirvana equals Samsara.' 'Emptiness is Form.' 'I am That.' 'Consciousness is All.' 'There are not two things.' 'Sat Chit Ananda.'

Every spiritual tradition has its own means of coming to this understanding, which is not just an intellectual understanding, but rather a Knowingness that is beyond the mind. And within each tradition itself there are as many variations on each approach as there are students.

This book explores what it is that is truly experienced. "What is the nature of our experience in this moment?" is the question that is returned to again and again.

However, this is not a philosophical treatise. It is a collection of contemplations and conversations in which a few core ideas are explored over and over again, each time from a slightly different angle, and for this reason there is an inevitable element of repetition.

In some ways this book is written like a piece of music in which a single theme is explored, questioned, modulated and restated. However, each time the central theme is returned to, it will, hopefully, have gathered depth and resonance due to the preceding contemplation.

The meaning of the words is not in the words themselves. Their meaning is in the contemplation from which they arise and to which they point. The text, therefore, is laid out with lots of space in order to encourage a contemplative approach.

Having said that, the conclusions drawn are only meant to uproot the old, conventional and dualistic formulations that have become so deeply embedded in the way we seem to experience ourselves and the world.

Once these old formulations have been uprooted, they do not need to be abandoned. They can still be used as provisional ideas that have a function to play in certain aspects of life.

The new formulations are perhaps closer or more accurate expressions of our experience than the old ones, but their purpose is not to replace the old certainties with new ones.

They simply lead to an open Unknowingness, which can be formulated from moment to moment in response to a given situation, including a question about the nature of experience.

There are many ways to come to this open Unknowingness, and the dismantling of our false certainties through investigation is just one of them that is offered here.

If our attention were now to be drawn to the white paper on which these words are written, we would experience the uncanny sensation of suddenly becoming aware of something that we simultaneously realise is so obvious as to require no mention. And yet at the moment when the paper is indicated, we seem to experience something new.

We have the strangely familiar experience of becoming aware of something which we were in fact already aware of. We become aware of being aware of the paper.

The paper is not a new experience that is created by this indication. However, our awareness of the paper *seems* to be a new experience.

Now what about the awareness itself, which is aware of the paper? Is it not always present behind and within every experience, just as the paper is present behind and within the words on this page?

And when our attention is drawn to it, do we not have the same strange feeling of having been made aware of something that we were in fact always aware of, but had not noticed?

Is this awareness not the most intimate and obvious fact of our experience, essential to and yet independent of the particular qualities of each experience itself, in the same way that the paper is the most obvious fact of this page, essential to and yet independent of each word?

Is this awareness itself not the support and the substance of every experience in the same way that the paper is the support and the substance of every word?

Does anything new need to be added to this page in order to see the paper? Does anything new need to be added to this current experience in order to become aware of the awareness that is its support and substance?

When we return to the words, having noticed the paper, do we lose sight of the paper? Do we not now see the two, the apparent two, simultaneously as one? And did we not always already experience them as one, without realising it?

Likewise, having noticed the awareness behind and within each experience, do we lose sight of that awareness when we return the focus of our attention to the objective aspect of experience? Do we not now see the two, the apparent two, Awareness and its object, simultaneously as one? And has it not always been so?

Do the words themselves affect the paper? Does it matter to the paper what is said in the words? Does the content of each experience affect the awareness in which it appears?

Every word on this page is in fact only made of paper. It only expresses the nature of the paper, although it may describe the moon.

Every experience only expresses Awareness or Consciousness, although experience itself is infinitely varied.

Awareness or Consciousness is the open Unknowingness on which every experience is written.

It is so obvious that it is not noticed.

It is so close that it cannot be known as an object and yet is always known.

It is so intimate that every experience, however tiny or vast, is utterly saturated and permeated with its presence.

It is so loving that all things possible of being imagined are contained unconditionally within it.

It is so open that it receives all things into itself.

It is so spacious and unlimited that everything is contained within it.

It is so present that every single experience is vibrating with its substance.

It is only this open Unknowingness, the source, the substance and the destiny of all experience, that is indicated here, over and over and over again.

Rupert Spira
October 2008

The Garden Of Unknowing

The abstract concepts of the mind cannot apprehend Reality although they are an expression of it.

Duality, the subject/object polarization, is inherent in the concepts of the mind. For instance, when we speak of the 'body' we refer to an object, which in turn implies a subject. If we explore this object we discover that it is non-existent as such and is in fact only a 'sensation'.

However, a 'sensation' is still an object and further exploration reveals that it is in fact made of 'sensing,' of 'mind stuff,' rather than anything physical.

However, 'sensing' in turn is discovered to be made of 'knowing.' And if we explore 'knowing' we find that it is made of Consciousness.

If we explore Consciousness we find that it has no objective qualities. And yet it is what we most intimately know ourselves to be. It is what we refer to as 'I.'

And if we explore 'I' we find it is made of...

The abstract concepts of the mind collapse here. They cannot go any further. There is no adequate name for that into which the mind dissolves. We are taken to the utmost simplicity of direct experience.

This de-objectification is the process of apparent *involution* through which That-Which-Cannot-Be-Named withdraws its projection of the mind, body and world, and rediscovers that it is the sole substance of the seamless totality of experience.

That-Which-Cannot-Be-Named, the Absolute Emptiness into which the mind collapses, then projects itself, *within itself*, back along the same path of apparent objectification, to recreate the appearance of the mind, body and world.

That-Which-Cannot-Be-Named, and yet which is sometimes referred to as 'I,' Consciousness, Being, Knowingness, takes the shape of thinking, sensing or perceiving in order to appear as a mind, a body or a world.

This is the process of apparent *evolution* through which That-Which-Cannot-Be-Named gives birth to a mind, a body and a world, without ever becoming anything other than itself.

This process of evolution and involution is the dance of Oneness, That-Which-Cannot-Be-Named taking shape and dissolving, vibrating in every nuance of experience and dissolving itself into itself, transparent, open, empty and luminous.

Mind attempts to describe the modulations of this emptiness manifesting itself as the fullness of experience and this fullness recognising itself as emptiness, knowing all the time that in doing so it is holding a candle to the wind.

Mind describes the names and forms through which That-Which-Cannot-Be-Named refracts itself, in order to make itself appear as two, as many, in order to make Consciousness/Being appear as Consciousness *and* Being.

And using the same names and forms, mind describes the apparent process through which That-Which-Cannot-Be-Named discovers that it never *becomes* anything, that it is always only itself and itself and itself.

Each statement that is made here is provisionally true in relation to one statement but false in relation to another. However, it is never *absolutely* true.

The purpose of every statement is to indicate the falsity of the previous one, only to await its own imminent demise.

Each is an agent of Truth, but never true.

Mind, in the broadest sense of the word*, is made of concepts and appearances. It never frames or grasps Reality itself.

However, by speaking in this way, mind is being used to create *evocations* rather than *descriptions* of the experience of Consciousness knowing itself.

These evocations are temporary expressions of That-Which-Cannot-Be-Named, like flowers blossoming for a moment, shedding the perfume of their origin on the Garden of Unknowing.

---

*The word 'mind' is used in two ways in this book. The first, as in this sentence, includes (a) thinking and imagining, (b) sensing (referring to bodily sensations) and (c) perceiving (referring to seeing, hearing, tasting, smelling and touching, through which the world is 'known'). In this case the body and the world are understood to be projections of the mind. The second refers only to thinking and imagining. In most cases the latter meaning is intended, but occasionally mind is referred to in its broader meaning.

Clear Seeing

All that is happening in these contemplations is the clear seeing of the essential nature of experience. There is no attempt to change or manipulate it, to create a peaceful or happy state, to get rid of suffering or to change the world. There is simply the clear seeing of the true nature of this current experience.

This clear seeing is not an intellectual understanding, although it may be formulated provisionally in intellectual terms when required by the current situation. Rather, it is the direct, intimate and immediate knowing of ourselves resting in and as the formless expanse of Presence, and simultaneously dancing in the vibrancy and aliveness of every gesture and nuance of the body, mind and world.

The clear seeing of what is has a profound effect on the appearance of the mind, the body and the world, but that is not the object of this investigation. There is no object to this investigation.

Even the purpose of 'seeing clearly' turns out to be too much in the end. It is the thorn that removes the thorn, and when even this last trace of becoming has been dissolved in understanding, it too is abandoned, leaving only Being.

However, in most cases this exploration is a prelude to the revelation of Being. We start with experience and stay close to it. We do not start with a theory, a model, a map or a teaching, and then try to fit our experience into that model. Absolutely nothing is taken for granted.

We start with experience and we end with experience. We allow the naked clarity of experience itself to relieve itself of the burden of duality.

We simply look at the facts of experience. "Is it true of my experience in this moment?" That is the only reference point.

The few core beliefs and preconceived ideas that we hold about the nature of ourselves and the world are exposed in this disinterested investigation. We do not do anything to these beliefs. We are not trying to destroy them but rather to expose them.

Belief and doubt are two sides of the same coin. When a belief is exposed it is found either to be true, in which case the belief becomes a fact and the doubt that was implicit in it is dissolved, or it is found to be false, in which case both the belief and the doubt will naturally come to an end.

Any feelings or patterns of behaviour that were dependent on the belief that has been exposed will, in due time, naturally dissolve, simply because they are no longer nourished by the belief. They die of neglect.

These feelings and patterns of behaviour are the counterpart at the level of the body to beliefs at the level of the mind, and their dissolution is accomplished in the same way. What was an investigation at the level of the mind, is an exploration at the level of the body.

In this exploration these feelings and patterns of behaviour are exposed, and in this exposure, their power to separate is revealed to be non-existent. Separation is not simply *understood* to be an illusion. It is *felt* as such.

No longer nourished by belief, these feelings are exposed and, as such, are seen for what they are. They die of the fierce clarity of being clearly seen.

This dissolution of beliefs and feelings has a profound effect on our lives, our ideas, our relationships, our bodies, our work, the world, in fact on everything.

However, the purpose of this investigation and exploration is not to change anything. It is simply the clear seeing of what is, and clear seeing is the shrine on which Being shines.

This line of investigation could be likened to taking several MRI scans of an apple. With each scan the apple is sliced up in different ways, each one showing a new section or point of view.

However, the apple is never touched in this process. It always remains just as it is, whole, untouched, unmodified, undivided. It only appears to be divided, and this appearance gives a more complete picture of its true undivided nature.

It is the same with our experience. The contemplations in this book are like MRI scans of our experience. They look at experience from many angles, spreading it out, opening it up. However, our experience itself is always one.

It is always a seamless, unified totality with no separate parts, and its nature is always only pure Consciousness. That is a fact of experience and it never changes, even if we think it to be otherwise.

This line of enquiry comes from the truth of direct experience and therefore leads back to it. It leads to the Reality of experience, to the experience of Consciousness knowing itself, knowingly. It is ruthless and tender at the same time, and utterly simple.

It is sometimes thought that this kind of enquiry is intellectual and abstract and seems to bear little relation to our day to day experience. However, it is only because our conventional dualistic concepts about the nature of Reality are themselves so densely interwoven with abstract and erroneous ideas that they require some meticulous deconstruction.

In this case it has not yet been seen that what are considered to be our normal, common sense assumptions, are in fact themselves intellectual and abstract – that is, they have little to do with the facts of experience.

By the end of the book I hope it will be clear that it is in fact our conventional ways of seeing that bear little relation to our actual moment by moment experience.

And, by contrast, I hope that the formulations expressed here will be understood as simple and obvious statements about the nature of our experience, albeit within the limited confines of the mind.

For instance, it is usually considered a fact of indisputable common sense that the body and the world exist as physical objects in time and space, independent and separate from Consciousness. Any line of reasoning that suggests that this is not the case, that there may be only the experience of Consciousness knowing itself in and as objects, is sometimes considered to be intellectual and abstract.

However, it is precisely the idea that the body and the world exist as objects in time and space, independent and separate from Consciousness, that is intellectual and abstract. It is not based on experience. And by the same token, the idea that there is only the experience of Consciousness knowing itself in and as objects, becomes a self-evident, obvious and indisputable fact of experience.

Of course the *appearance* of physical objects continues, but appearance is no longer mistaken for Reality.

However, it would be a misunderstanding to think that appearances have to disappear for Reality to be revealed. It is simply that the misinterpretation is no longer superimposed onto experience.

The body and the world continue to appear in the same way, but it is clearly seen that the experience of the appearance of the body and the world takes place simultaneously with the experience of Consciousness knowing itself. It is the same experience, one experience.

The experience of Consciousness knowing itself knowingly in and as all appearances, becomes as obvious and self-evident as the previous, apparently obvious and self-evident experience of objects existing in time and space, independent and separate from Consciousness.

What Truly Is

Whatever it is that is seeing and understanding these words, is what is referred to here as 'Consciousness.' It is what we know ourselves to be, what we refer to as 'I.'

Everything that is known is known *through* Consciousness. Therefore whatever is known is only as good as our knowledge of Consciousness.

What do we know about Consciousness?

We know that Consciousness *is*, and that everything is known *by* and *through* it. However, Consciousness itself cannot be known as an object.

If Consciousness had any objective qualities that could be known, it would be the *Knower* of those qualities, and would therefore be independent of them. We cannot therefore know anything objective about Consciousness.

Therefore, if we do not know *what* Consciousness is, what 'I' am, but we know *that* it is, and if everything that we experience is known *through* or *by* this knowing Consciousness, how can we know what *anything* really is?

All we can know for sure about an object is that it *is*, and that quality of 'isness' is what is referred to here as Being or Existence. It is that part of our experience that is real, that lasts, that is not a fleeting appearance. It is also therefore referred to as its Reality.

We know that Consciousness is present now and we know that whatever it is that is being experienced in this moment, exists. It has Existence.

If we think that we know something objective about ourselves or the world, then whatever that something is that we think we know, will condition our subsequent enquiry into the nature of experience. So before knowing what something is, if that is possible, we must first come to the understanding that we do *not* know what anything really is.

Therefore the investigation into the nature of ourselves and of the world of objects initially has more to do with the exposure of deeply held ideas and beliefs about the way we think things are, than of acquiring any new knowledge. It is the exposure of our false certainties.

Once a belief that we previously held to be a fact is exposed as such, it drops away naturally. Whether or not something further than the exposure of our false ideas about the nature things needs to be accomplished, remains to be seen. We cannot know that until all false ideas have been removed.

Many of our ideas and beliefs about ourselves and the world are so deeply ingrained that we are unaware that they are beliefs and take them, without questioning, for the absolute truth.

For instance, we believe that we are a body, that we are a man or a woman and that we were born and will die. We believe that we are an entity amongst innumerable other entities, and that this entity resides somewhere in the body, usually behind the eyes or in the chest area.

We believe that we are the subject of our experience and that everything and everyone else is the object. We believe that we, as this subject, are the doer of our actions, the thinker of our thoughts, the feeler of our feelings, the chooser of our choices. We believe that this entity we consider ourselves to be, has freedom of choice over some aspects of experience but not others.

We believe that time and space are actually experienced, that they existed before we did and will continue to do so after we have died.

We believe that objects exist independent of their being perceived, that Consciousness is personal and limited, that it is a by-product of the mind and that mind is a by-product of the body.

These and many other such beliefs are considered to be so obviously true that they are beyond the need of questioning. They amount to a religion of materialism to which the vast majority of humanity subscribes. This is especially surprising in areas of life that purport to deal explicitly with questions about the nature of Reality, such as religion, philosophy and art.

The only field available for enquiry is experience itself. This may seem almost too obvious to mention, but its implications are profound. It implies that we never experience anything *outside* experience. If there *is* something outside experience, we have absolutely no knowledge of it, and therefore cannot legitimately assert that it exists.

This in turn implies that if we are to make an honest investigation into the nature of Reality, we have to discard any presumptions that are not derived from direct experience. Any such presumptions will not relate to experience itself and will therefore not relate to ourselves or the world. If we honestly stick to our experience, we will be surprised to find how many of our assumptions and presumptions turn out to be untenable beliefs.

All experience takes place here and now, so the nature of Reality, whatever that is, must be present in the intimacy and immediacy of this current experience.

'I,' Consciousness, is present, and *something*, these words, the sound of the traffic, a feeling of sadness, whatever it is, is also present.

We do not know what this Consciousness is. Nor do we know what the Reality of these words or the current experience is. However, there is the *Consciousness* of something and there is the *Existence* of that something. Both are present in this current experience.

What is the relationship between them?

The mind has built a powerful edifice of concepts about Reality that bears little relation to actual experience and, as a result, Consciousness has veiled itself from itself. These concepts are built out of mind and therefore their deconstruction is one of the ways through which Consciousness comes to recognise itself again – that is, to know itself again.

Consciousness is in fact always knowing itself. However, through this deconstruction of concepts, Consciousness comes to recognise itself, not through the reflected veil of apparent objects, but knowingly and directly.

Concepts are not destroyed in this process. They are still available for use when needed.

In the contemplations that comprise this book it is acknowledged that the purpose of reasoning is not to frame or apprehend Reality. However, it is also acknowledged that the mind has constructed complex and persuasive ideas that have posited an image of ourselves and of the world that is very far from the facts of our experience.

These ideas have convinced us that there is a world that exists separate from and independent of Consciousness. They have persuaded us to believe that 'I', the Consciousness that is seeing these words, is an entity that resides inside the body, that it was born and will die, and that it is the *subject* of experience whilst everything else, the world, 'other,' is the *object*.

Although this is never our actual experience, the mind is so persuasive and convincing, that we have duped ourselves into believing that we actually experience these two elements, that we experience the world separate and apart from our Self, and that we experience our own Self as a separate and independent Consciousness.

In the disinterested contemplation of our experience we measure the facts of experience itself against these beliefs.

The falsity of the ideas that the mind entertains about the nature of Reality, about the nature of experience, is exposed in this disinterested contemplation.

All spiritual traditions acknowledge that Reality cannot be apprehended with the mind. As a result of this understanding some teachings have denied the use of the mind as a valid tool of enquiry or exploration.

It is true that Consciousness is beyond the mind and cannot therefore be framed within its abstract concepts. However this does not invalidate the use of the mind to explore the nature of Consciousness and Reality.

Ignorance is composed of beliefs and belief is already an activity of mind. If we deny the validity of mind, why use it in the first place to harbour beliefs?

By reading these words, we are, consciously or unconsciously, agreeing to accept the validity and, by the same token, the limitations of the mind.

We are giving the mind credibility in spite of its limitations. We are acknowledging its ability to play a part in drawing attention to that which is beyond itself or outside the sphere of its knowledge.

It would be disingenuous to use the mind to deny its own validity. Our very use of the mind asserts its validity. However, it is a different matter to use the mind to understand its own limits.

It may well be that at the end of a process of exploring the nature of experience, using the full capacity of its powers of conceptual thinking, the mind will come to understand the limits of its ability to apprehend the truth of the matter and, as a result, will spontaneously come to an end. It will collapse from within, so to speak.

However, this is a very different situation from one in which the mind has been denied any provisional credibility on the basis that nothing it says about Reality can ultimately be true.

As a result of the exposure of beliefs and feelings that derive from preconceived, unsubstantiated notions of Reality, a new invitation opens up, another possibility is revealed.

This possibility cannot be apprehended by the mind because it is beyond the mind. However, the obstacles to this new possibility are revealed and dissolved in this investigation.

They are dissolved by our openness to the possibility that in this moment we actually experience only one thing, that experience is not divided into 'I' and other, subject and object, me and the world, Consciousness and Existence.

We are open to the possibility that there is only one single, seamless totality, that Consciousness and Existence are one, that there is only *one* Reality.

The edifice of dualistic ideas, which *seems* to be validated by experience, is well constructed with beliefs at the level of the mind and feelings at the level of the body, which are tightly interwoven, mutually substantiating and validating one another.

In the disinterested contemplation of these ideas and feelings their falsity is unraveled. We see clearly that our ideas do not correspond to our experience. This paves the way for experience to reveal itself to us as it truly is, as in fact it always is, free from the ignorance of dualistic thinking.

We begin to experience ourselves and the world as they truly are.

Our experience itself does not change but we *feel* that it changes. Reality remains as it always is, for it is what it is, independent of the ideas we entertain about it.

However, our *interpretation* changes and this new interpretation becomes the cornerstone of a new possibility.

This new possibility comes from an unknown direction. It does not come as an object, a thought or a feeling. It is unveiled, in most cases, as a series of revelations, each dismantling part of the previous edifice of dualistic thinking.

And the unfolding of this revelation, in turn, has a profound impact on the appearance of the mind, the body and the world.

Consciousness veils itself from itself by pretending to limit itself to a separate entity and then forgets that it is pretending.

As a corollary to this self-limitation, Consciousness projects all that is not this 'separate self,' outside of itself. This projection is what we call 'the world.' And thus the separation between 'I' and 'the world' is born.

In reality this separation has never taken place. If we look for it, we can never actually find it. Ignorance is an illusion. It is an illusion that is wrought through the conceptual powers of the mind, through erroneous beliefs.

These beliefs are created and maintained through a process of deluded thinking – that is, by thinking that bears no relation to actual experience. The dissolution of these beliefs is accomplished by exploring and exposing them, using direct experience as the guiding reference.

Nothing new is created by this process of exploration. Its purpose is not enlightenment or self-realisation. It is simply to see clearly what is.

Our beliefs are the root cause of psychological suffering and they are dismantled by a process of contemplative investigation.

What we normally consider to be a line of investigation begins with assumptions that are considered to be implicitly true. In this contemplation we start with the same assumptions, but we measure them against the truth of our experience. We do not build on them, we deconstruct them.

This line of reasoning leads to understanding. However, understanding does not take place in the mind. It is beyond the mind. It is a moment when Consciousness experiences itself directly and knowingly.

Understanding is not *created* by a process in the mind any more than blue sky is created by a clearing in the clouds. However, it may be *revealed* by it.

Understanding is often preceded by a line of enquiry and can subsequently be formulated by the mind. Such a formulation, that comes from understanding and not from concepts, has the power to take us to the experience of Reality.

Through its reasoning powers the mind is brought to its own limit and, as a result, the edifice of mind collapses. This is the experience of understanding, the timeless moment in which Consciousness is revealed to itself.

Consciousness perceives itself. It knows itself, knowingly.

Everything Falls Into Place

I, this Consciousness that is seeing these words and experiencing whatever it is that is being experienced in this moment, is not located inside a mind. The mind is not located inside a body and the body is not located inside a world.

The body is simply the *sensation* of the body and the world is simply the *perception* of the world.

Take away sensing and perceiving from the experience of the body and the world and what objective qualities are left of them? None!

Sensations and perceptions are made out of mind – that is, they are made out of sensing and perceiving.

There is no other substance to them other than sensing and perceiving.

If there was another substance, independent of sensing and perceiving, that constituted the body and the world, that substance would remain after sensing and perceiving had been withdrawn.

However, nothing objective remains of the experience of the body and the world when sensing and perceiving have been withdrawn.

And if we look clearly at the substance of mind, the substance of perceiving and sensing, we find that it is none other than the Consciousness in which it appears.

If there was another substance, apart from Consciousness, that constituted the mind, then that substance would remain after Consciousness had been withdrawn from the experience of the mind. However, when Consciousness is withdrawn from the mind, the mind vanishes absolutely, leaving only Consciousness.

17

The mind, the body and the world are located *inside* Consciousness and they are made only *out of* Consciousness. That is our experience.

This is not a new experience that is arrived at through enquiry or meditation. It has always been our experience. We just may not have noticed it. In meditation we simply notice that this is always, already the case.

If we try to perceive this perceiving Consciousness as an object we find that it is impossible.

Take the analogy of Consciousness as space, and imagine that this space, like Consciousness, is conscious, aware, that it has the capacity to see, to perceive, to experience, that it is an 'experiencing space.'

Now imagine what this space would perceive if it were to look *for* itself, if it were to look *at* itself.

It would not see anything objective, because space cannot be perceived. It is empty, transparent, colourless and invisible. This perceiving space is too close to itself to be able to see itself.

The space that is being looked for is the space that is looking.

Only an object can be perceived objectively, so this perceiving space would see only the objects that were present within it, but not the space itself.

However, we have said that this space is, like Consciousness, endowed with the capacity to experience, that it is an 'experiencing space.' So to look *for* itself is unnecessary because it is, by definition, *already* perceiving itself. It is already experiencing itself, because that is what it is. Its nature is 'experiencing.'

18

Its being itself *is* the knowing or experiencing of itself.

However, the experience of 'experiencing itself' is colourless, transparent and invisible. It has no objective qualities. There is nothing that is being *objectively* experienced.

And because this conscious space is accustomed to experiencing 'objects,' it construes this non-objective experience of itself, this colourless, transparent, invisible experience, as a non-experience. It thinks that itself, this conscious space, is not present.

At this point there are three options for this space:

One is to search for itself as an objective experience, not understanding that it is already experiencing itself and cannot therefore ever find itself anywhere else.

The second is to identify itself with some of the objects that are present and thereby satisfy the sense of identity that is inherent within itself. In this way it mixes up its own identity with an object.

The third is to see clearly that it is already only experiencing itself and always has been.

Whatever is seen or perceived is an object, an object of the mind, body or world.

Whatever is perceived is not this perceiving Consciousness. It is an object that is appearing *to* it, *within* it.

If Consciousness cannot be perceived as an object, how do we know that it has a limit?

Do we *experience* a limit to this perceiving Consciousness?

It is impossible to experience a limit to Consciousness because such a limit would, by definition, have some objective quality.

Such an apparent limit would have to be an object and, like all objects, would itself appear *within* Consciousness. Consciousness would be *aware* of it, but would not be *defined* by it.

In fact an object that appears within Consciousness tells us nothing about Consciousness other than that it is present and aware, that it *is*, just as a chair tells us that the space in which it appears, is present.

Therefore we have no actual experience of a limit to Consciousness.

And if there is no experiential evidence to suggest that Consciousness is limited, on what grounds do we believe that it is personal? Why do we think that we, Consciousness, are a personal entity inside the body?

Thoughts are limited. Bodies are limited. The world is limited. However, there is no experiential evidence to validate the belief that Consciousness, in which the mind, the body and the world appear, is limited or personal.

If we claim that Consciousness has a limit there must, by definition, be an experience of that limit, and therefore of that which exists *outside* that limit, of something that *borders* Consciousness.

However, how could we have an experience of such an object, if that object were itself outside the limit of Consciousness? How could we be conscious of something beyond Consciousness?

Consciousness is required for every experience and therefore, by definition, it is not possible to experience something outside Consciousness. And if we do not experience such an object, how can we say that anything exists outside Consciousness?

We have no experience of the existence of anything outside Consciousness and therefore we have no experience of a limited or personal Consciousness.

Consciousness is transparent, colourless, Self-luminous, Self-experiencing, Self-knowing, Self-evident. That is our experience in this moment.

Consciousness is known as Omnipresence, because there is nowhere where Consciousness is not. It is not that Consciousness is everywhere. It is that every 'where' is *in* Consciousness.

Consciousness is known as Omniscience, because whatever is known is known *by* and *through* Consciousness. It knows all that is known.

It is known as Omnipotence, because whatever appears depends solely on Consciousness for its Existence. Whatever appears emerges *out of*, is sustained *by* and is dissolved *into*, Consciousness. Consciousness creates everything out of it own Being.

Consciousness cannot be known by the mind. The mind is an object. It does not know anything. It is itself known by Consciousness.

Therefore Consciousness cannot be described by the mind. The images and metaphors that are used in these contemplations are not *descriptions* of Consciousness. They are *evocations* of Consciousness.

They are evocations of the non-objective experience of Consciousness knowing itself, the experience of Consciousness recognizing itself, remembering itself.

They are invitations from Consciousness to Consciousness, to be *knowingly* itself.

If we have no experience of a limit or a boundary to Consciousness, if we have no experience of a personal Consciousness, how do we know that the Consciousness 'in you' and the Consciousness 'in me' are different? There is no evidence in our experience to suggest that we have different Consciousnesses, indeed that there is more than one Consciousness.

Mind can know nothing of Consciousness and yet at the same time, all that is known through mind, *is* the Knowingness of Consciousness.

Consciousness cannot frame or define itself within the limits of mind, although everything that appears in mind is its expression.

We make this investigation and come to the understanding that there is no experiential evidence of a separate, personal, limited Consciousness. That is as far as the mind can go.

In coming to this deep conviction, we open ourselves to another possibility, the possibility that there is only one Consciousness. We explore and experiment with this new possibility in our lives, and it is the response we get from the universe in actual experience, that is the confirmation of this possibility.

As this conviction becomes deeper and deeper, so the confirmation from the universe becomes more and more obvious. Everything falls into place.

Like a landscape that appears gradually out of the mist without our doing anything to bring it about, so it becomes more and more obvious, without our doing anything about it, that we, Consciousness, have only ever been experiencing our own unlimited Self and that the experience of the world is the revelation of our own infinite and eternal Being.

The very best that the mind can do is to explore its own limits and come to the conclusion that it does not and cannot know what anything really is.

However, this is a manner of speaking. There is no mind. Mind is simply the current thought, if there is a current thought. And a current thought cannot do anything or explore anything, any more than a lamppost can do or explore anything.

So when we say the mind can explore its own limits we are using conventional dualistic language. However, it should not be concluded from this that the implicitly dualistic presumptions that are encoded in our language are being condoned here.

When we say that the mind can explore its limits we are really saying that Consciousness, the Knowingness that *is* Consciousness, takes the shape of abstract thinking and, through this shape, explores its own capacity to represent itself in the abstract terms of thought.

In doing so it discovers that the abstract concepts of mind do not represent its own direct, intimate experience of itself.

It is the exploration and the subsequent discovery that Consciousness cannot be found or represented by mind, by thinking, which truly brings this search for itself in the mind to an end.

As the mind, as seeking and thinking, comes to an end, that which is ever-present as the support and the substance of the mind, is revealed.

This is the experience of understanding. It is a non-objective experience and is therefore timeless.

However, this revelation is not *caused* by the cessation of mind, any more than light is caused by the cessation of darkness. It is the line of enquiry that brings the mind to its natural ending and, as the mind dissolves, that which understands it, that which 'stands under' it, is revealed.

During the appearance of mind, That-Which-Is-Ever-Present *is* the substance of that appearance and yet is apparently disguised as such. In this case Consciousness fails to recognize itself.

However, once this understanding, this Self-recognition, has taken place, Consciousness no longer needs to forget itself during the appearance of the mind (or the body or the world). It recognizes itself *in* and *as* the activity of the mind as well as in its absence.

What it is that brings about this Self-recognition is a mystery. It is like looking in the mirror and exclaiming, "Oh, it's me!"

Having said that, with this Self-recognition comes the felt understanding that Consciousness has always only ever been experiencing itself. It becomes obvious that no new experience has taken place.

It is understood that the experience of knowing itself, and *only* that experience, has always been taking place and therefore it does not make sense to ascribe a cause to something that has always been present.

To look for a cause of this Self-recognition, just as to look for a reason for it, is itself the very denial of this Self-recognition, and yet that denial is in turn the shape that this ever-present Self-recognition is taking at that moment.

How can that which is the cause of all things be said to have a cause? What could cause Consciousness, if everything that might be a candidate for being such a cause, is itself caused *by* Consciousness?

Consciousness is its own cause, which is the same as saying that it is causeless.

Abide As You Are

Meditation is simply to abide as oneself.

We remain as we are and allow the mind, the body and the world to appear and disappear without interference. If there is interference, then that is understood to be part of the mind's activity and is allowed to be exactly as it is.

Our objective experience consists of thoughts and images, which we call the mind; sensations, which we call the body; and sense perceptions, which we call the world. In fact we do not experience a mind, a body or a world as such. We experience thinking, sensing and perceiving.

In fact all that we perceive are our perceptions. We have no evidence that a world exists outside our perception of it. We do not perceive a world 'out there.' We perceive our *perception* of the world and all perception takes places in Consciousness.

In meditation we simply allow this thinking/sensing/perceiving to be whatever it is from moment to moment. This thinking/sensing/ perceiving is always moving, always changing. We simply allow it to flow through us, to appear, to remain and to disappear. In fact that is all that is happening anyway.

That in which the thinking/sensing/perceiving appears, is what we call 'I'. It is the conscious, witnessing Presence, which experiences whatever it is that is being experienced from moment to moment.

There is no need to make this witnessing Presence conscious. It is already so. There is no need to make it peaceful. It is already so. There is no need to wake it up. It is always, already awake. There is no need to make it unlimited and impersonal. It is already so.

And there is no need to make the mind, the body and the world peaceful. They are always moving and changing.

We remain as we are and we allow the mind, the body and the world to be as they are.

As we do so, the mind, the body and the world gradually return to their true place and their nature is revealed. We see that in fact they never left their true place, that they were never anything other than what they truly are. We simply stop imagining that they are distant, separate and other and, as a result, they stop appearing as such.

Imagine a room filled with people conversing. In this metaphor the space of the room is this conscious, witnessing Presence that we call 'I'. The people are thoughts and images, bodily sensations and world perceptions.

There are all sorts of people in the room, large, small, kind, unkind, intelligent, unintelligent, loud, quiet, friendly, unfriendly, etc... a complex diversity of characters, moving, changing, interacting, appearing and disappearing, each doing their own thing.

What does the behaviour of these people matter to the space of the room? Does the space have anything to gain or lose by trying to change any of the people? Is the space itself changed when one of the people changes?

The space is independent of the people, although the people are dependent on the space. The space is present before the people arrive, it is present during their stay and it is present when they depart. In fact it is present before the building was constructed and it will be present after it is demolished. It is always present.

The same is true of Consciousness. Whatever is being experienced in this moment is taking place within Consciousness, and Consciousness itself remains as it is at all times, unmodified, unchanged, unconcerned.

Consciousness is what we are, and to be as we are is the highest form of meditation. All other meditations are simply a modulation of this meditation of *abidance as we are*.

To begin with, meditation may seem to be something that we do, but later we discover that it is simply what we are. It is the natural condition of all beings.

It cannot be brought about because it is already the case. It cannot be attained because it is what we always, already are. It cannot be lost for there is nowhere for it to go.

We simply allow everything to be as it is. As we allow everything to be as it is, we are, unknowingly at first, taking our stand in our true nature. In fact we have never left our true nature but now we begin to reside there knowingly.

At some stage it dawns on us that 'I' does not *abide* in its true nature. Who is there to abide in something other than itself? It simply *is* that. We simply *are* that and always have been.

Even to say *'always'* is not quite right, because 'always' implies an infinite extension in time. The idea of an infinite extension of time appears *in* the 'I,' in Consciousness, from time to time, but the 'I' never appears in an infinite extension of time.

It just *is*. 'I,' Consciousness, just *am*.

The Drop Of Milk

Our experience consists of that which is known and that which knows. It is not just the world, but also the body and the mind that are known.

The world is known so it cannot be the Knower. It cannot be that which knows. The body and the mind are also known, so they cannot be that which knows. The world, the body and the mind are *experienced*, so they cannot be that which *experiences*.

Whenever the body, the mind and the world are present, they are *known*. That which *knows* the body, the mind and the world, is present during their appearance *and* their absence.

That which is known cannot be the Knower and the Knower cannot be known objectively.

Normally we are only aware of the known, but when attention is drawn to the presence of the Knower, to that which knows and experiences, whatever that is, it immediately becomes obvious that there is something present that is conscious of the body, the mind and the world.

As we do this, whatever it is that knows seems suddenly to become more present. It shines.

In fact it is simply discovered to have been always present, but apparently eclipsed by our exclusive focus on the known.

The Knower is Consciousness. It is that which knows and experiences. It is this Consciousness that we refer to when we say, 'I.'

When it is said, "We give our attention to that which is known," it means that it is 'I,' Consciousness, that gives its attention to that which is known.

When it is said, "We give our attention instead to the Knower," it means that 'I,' Consciousness, gives its attention to itself.

Of course Consciousness is already itself. It does not need to give itself attention.

So when it is said, "We give our attention to the Knower, to Consciousness," it means in practice that 'I,' Consciousness, withdraws its attention from its exclusive focus on the known, on objects.

In doing so Consciousness is, without knowing it to begin with, naturally 'returning to itself,' which means it is becoming aware of itself. It doesn't actually return to itself, because it never left itself. It is never not aware of itself.

Even when Consciousness is exclusively focused on objects, it never leaves itself. It just seems to forget itself from time to time. It seems to ignore itself.

However, even in ignoring itself, something is known and that knowing *is* the Knowingness of Consciousness knowing itself. Hence there is never any real ignorance.

For this reason, there is no answer to the question as to the cause or reason for ignorance. How can there be a cause or a reason for something that is non-existent?

We cannot answer the question 'Why?' because the question itself *creates* the ignorance about which it is asking. It apparently creates time, cause and effect and, therefore, the appearance of 'two things,' which are themselves found to be non-existent when the nature of experience is clearly seen.

At the same time Consciousness knows itself in the very knowing of this question. How then can apparent ignorance be said to be truly ignorant? It cannot.

When Consciousness looks for itself, it merges with itself. It is revealed to itself and this revelation is the dissolution of the question. It is this Knowingness beyond the mind that is the true answer to all questions about the true nature of experience.

Consciousness pretends to be other than it is and then, as that apparent other, it looks for itself. Of course, it can never find itself as an object because it already is itself, just as the eye cannot see itself.

However, it does not *need* to find itself because it already *is* itself. All that is required is to stop pretending that it is not itself.

What to the apparent other is a process of searching, is to Consciousness simply the process of discovering that it always already knows itself.

The mind is a series of abstract concepts that appear within Consciousness. Every thought is an object and therefore the objectless Consciousness in which thoughts appear can never itself appear as a thought.

All thoughts are objects. Therefore, it is impossible to think of Consciousness.

When we think of anything other than Consciousness (or Truth or Reality or whatever word is used) we end up with a concept, an idea of that thing, which is not the thing *itself*. It is a *representation* of that thing in the mind's code – that is, it is a concept.

However, the thought about Consciousness or Reality is unique amongst all thoughts. When we try to think of Consciousness, it is like looking into a black hole. It is not even black. The mind simply cannot go there. It cannot go to that objectless place because the mind is itself an object. How could an object fit into a space that has no dimensions?

So as the mind tries to turn itself towards Consciousness, it dissolves. It is consumed in what is, from its own point of view, the nothing-ness of Consciousness. However, its dissolution is the revelation of Presence, the revelation of that in which thought dissolves.

So the thought about Consciousness is unique in that it does not lead to a concept, to a substitute for the thing itself, but rather to the *Reality* of Consciousness itself. It leads directly to its referent, not to a symbol. It leads to the direct experience of Consciousness knowing itself, knowingly.

Nothing objective is known in this placeless place of Consciousness.

It is a knowing but not a knowing of *something*. It is pure Knowing-ness.

The seeking thought, which looks for Consciousness, merges with Consciousness. It reveals Consciousness.

The seeking thought is like a sugar cube. Looking for Consciousness is like putting the sugar cube in a cup of tea. The tea dissolves the sugar cube. Likewise Consciousness dissolves the seeking thought.

A more accurate metaphor would be that of a drop of milk in a jar of water. The milk is essentially the same substance as the water, although it is coloured by a slight taint of objectivity. It is white, not colourless. As we watch the drop of milk, it expands into the water, losing its form by degrees, until it is utterly merged into the surrounding water.

Such is the thought that seeks Consciousness, that is directed towards Presence. It is essentially made out of the very same Consciousness that it is seeking, but it does not know this yet and hence there is some apparent differentiation between itself and Consciousness. It is opaque. It is not transparent.

As it searches for Consciousness, it becomes more and more like Consciousness, which means it loses its otherness, its opacity, its apparent objectivity.

The water, which was already present in the milk, loses its whiteness and remains as it is, as water.

This expansion of the drop of milk into the surrounding water is the process of refinement that our thoughts go through as we try to approach Consciousness. Consciousness cannot be found as a thought, so thought is gradually purified of its objectivity as it tries to find Consciousness.

A time comes when the thought gives up its last layer of objectivity and merges into Presence. In fact it is Presence that gradually gives up identification with subtler and subtler layers of objectivity, until it comes to recognize thought as its very own self.

The mind does not *find* Truth. It does not *find* Reality. It is *dissolved* in it.

The mind cannot *release* itself. It is itself *released* into the infinite expanse of Consciousness that is its ground.

Understanding is the *dissolution* of the mind into its support, into its ground. It is the experience of Consciousness knowing itself, returning to itself knowingly.

It is not an objective experience. It is the experience of *Knowing*. This experience is always present, whether objects are present or not.

We become what we think about.

We are both the subject and the object of the thought that seeks Consciousness.

For Consciousness, to know itself is to be itself and to be itself is to know itself.

Consciousness Shines In Every Experience

Meditation is not an activity. It is the cessation of an activity.

In the final analysis, nothing that is absolutely true can be said of meditation, not even that it is the cessation of an activity, because meditation takes place or, more accurately, is *present* beyond the mind and the mind therefore, by definition, has no access to it.

However, in order to understand that meditation is not an activity, we first come to the understanding that it is the *cessation* of an activity.

This understanding is a very efficient tool for undermining the belief that meditation is something that we *do*.

Once we have fully understood that meditation is not an activity, the activity that we previously considered to be meditation will naturally come to an end. At that point, the understanding that meditation is *not* an activity has fulfilled its purpose and can also be abandoned.

Once the thorn has removed the thorn, both are thrown away.

In order to understand that meditation is not an activity we can use the example of a clenched fist. If we take our open hand and slowly close it tightly, an effort is required both to clench the hand and to maintain it in that contracted gesture.

If we maintain the hand in this contracted gesture for some time, the muscles will become accustomed to this new position, and we will soon cease to be aware that a subtle effort is continually being applied in order to maintain it.

If someone were now to ask us to open our hand, we would feel that the opening of the hand required some effort. At some stage, as we open our hand, we will become aware of the fact that we are not applying a new effort in order to open the hand, but rather that we are *relaxing* a previous effort, of which we were no longer even aware.

The apparent effort to *open* the hand turns out to be the *relaxation* of the original effort to *contract* the hand. What appeared to be the *initiation* of an effort turns out to be the *cessation* of an effort.

Meditation works in a similar way. Our true nature is open, unlimited, free, conscious, self-luminous and self-evident. This is our moment by moment experience, although we may not be aware of it.

This open, free, unlimited Consciousness has contracted upon itself. It has seemingly shrunk itself into the narrow frame of a body and a mind, and limited itself to a tiny location in a vast space and into a brief moment in an endless expanse of time.

This is the primary self-contraction that open, free, unlimited Consciousness chooses from moment to moment of its own free will.

It draws a line within the seamless totality of its experience and says to itself, "I am this and not that," "I am here and not there," "I am me and not other."

Feeling itself isolated and therefore vulnerable and afraid, this open, free, unlimited Consciousness now sets about supporting and protecting its new self-imposed identity as a fragment.

To effect this it reinforces its boundaries with layer upon layer of contraction. At the level of the mind these contractions are made out of desires and addictions on the one hand, and resistances, fears and rejections on the other. These are the many faces of our likes and dislikes, the "I want" and the "I don't want."

At the level of the body these contractions are made out of bodily sensations with which Consciousness identifies itself. They are the apparent location of 'I' inside the body.

With each new layer of contraction this open, free, unlimited Consciousness forgets its own unlimited nature more and more profoundly, and in doing so throws a veil over itself. It hides itself from itself.

In spite of this there are frequent intrusions into its own self-generated isolation which remind itself of its real nature... the smile of a stranger, the cry of an infant, an unbearable grief, a brief desireless moment upon the fulfilment of a desire, a moment of humour, the peace of deep sleep, a pause in the thinking process, a memory of childhood, the transition between dreaming and waking, the recognition of beauty, the love of a friend, a glimpse of understanding.

These are moments that are offered to this now veiled presence of Consciousness, innumerable tastes of its own Freedom and Happiness, which remind it briefly of itself, before it is eclipsed again by the efficiency of the defences within which it has apparently confined itself.

In this way, with layer upon layer of self-contraction, Consciousness has reduced itself to a well-fortified, separate and vulnerable entity.

This is not an activity that took place sometime in the past and which is now irrevocably cast in stone. It is an activity that is taking place now, in this moment.

This open, free, unlimited Consciousness is, without knowing it, *doing* this very activity of separation. This activity defines the 'person,' the 'separate entity.'

The separate entity is something we, as Consciousness, *do*. It is not something we *are*.

As a result of Consciousness contracting upon itself and imagining itself to be a fragment in this way, it projects outside of itself everything that is not contained within the boundary of its own self-imposed and limited identity. The world now appears as 'outside' and 'other.' It becomes everything that 'Consciousness-as-a-fragment' is not.

And this world that now appears separate from and outside of Consciousness, seems to perfectly confirm Consciousness' new view of itself as a limited fragment. The world becomes the vast and potentially threatening container of this 'Consciousness-as-a-fragment.'

Ironically, it is precisely *because* the world is, in Reality, an appearance in Consciousness and an expression of it, that it so accurately reflects the ideas that Consciousness entertains about it.

If Consciousness believes itself to be a fragment, to be limited, to be bound and to appear in time and space, then the world will appear as the counterpart of that fragment.

Having denied itself its own birthright, its own eternal, all-pervading status, Consciousness confers this same status on the world of appearances. It bestows its own Reality on the world of appearances and in exchange appropriates for itself the fleeting, fragility of that world.

It forgoes its own Reality as the ground and nature of all experience, and instead projects it onto its own creation, onto the world of appearances.

Consciousness exchanges its nature with the world of appearances. It has no alternative but to do this.

In fact Consciousness never ceases to experience itself. Embedded within every experience is the taste of its own eternity.

However, having conceptualised itself into a limited and separate entity, it has to account for its own intimate experience of Presence, of Being, elsewhere, and hence confers it on the 'world,' on 'other.'

In this way, time and space *seem* to become the ground and substance of Reality, the 'sine qua non' of our experience, and Consciousness in turn *seems* to display the intermittent, limited, changing qualities that really belong to the world of appearances.

Consciousness forgets that it has done this, that it is doing this, and as a result the world seems to inherit the characteristics of Consciousness. The world *seems* to become like Consciousness, solid, real, permanent and substantial.

And in turn Consciousness *seems* to give up its own innate qualities and to assume those that rightfully belong to the world of appearances – that is, it *seems* to become fleeting, momentary, fragile and insubstantial.

In short, Consciousness creates an appearance that is consistent with its own beliefs.

In fact the 'belief-of-itself-as-a-limited-fragment' and the 'appearance-of-the-world-as-a-solid-and-separate-entity' are co-created as a seamless, mutually validating whole.

William Blake expressed the same understanding, "As a man is, so he sees." This could be expressed, "As Consciousness sees itself, so the world appears." It is an almost watertight conspiracy, wrought of the freedom and creativity of Consciousness itself.

However, it is the very same power that enables the world to appear in accordance with Consciousness' view of itself as a fragment, that in turn enables the world to appear in accordance with Consciousness' new view of itself, when it begins to awaken to its own Reality, when it begins to remember itself.

This is the magical nature of the world: that the same world can be seen to validate either ignorance or understanding. In fact, it is the magical nature of *Consciousness*, its creativity, its omnipotence, which makes this possible!

Whether we know it or not, we are always this open, free, unlimited Consciousness, and yet sometimes we forget this. It is our freedom to forget.

Once we have forgotten, no other freedom is available to us, save the freedom to remember again.

Although we are always this open, free, unlimited Consciousness, at times we seem to be limited. We *feel* limited. Consciousness experiences itself as being bound by it own projection.

Having projected a boundary within its own unlimitedness, Consciousness then identifies itself with that limitation. It forgets its real nature. It 'falls' into ignorance.

As a result, Consciousness then feels that its own true nature is somehow strange, unknown and unfamiliar, that it has been lost and needs to be found, that it has been forgotten and needs to be remembered, that it is elsewhere, other and apart.

Consciousness does not realise that it is already precisely what it is looking for, that it is already itself.

It does not see clearly that the very Knowingness of whatever it is that is known in any moment, *is* the knowing of itself.

However, no matter how deeply Consciousness identifies itself with a fragment of its own making, no matter how deep the ignorance and the subsequent thoughts, feelings and activities that are generated by this ignorance, no matter how successfully Consciousness conceals its own nature from itself, its memory of itself is always deeper than its forgetting.

This is always the case, simply by virtue of the fact that before Consciousness seems to become anything other than itself, it is still always only itself.

Consciousness is the primary experience in all experience, whatever the particular character of that experience. And for this reason, the search for itself, the desire to return to itself, to abide in itself, can never be extinguished.

And, ironically, it is for the very same reason that the search will be continually undermined, because when it is understood that Consciousness always only experiences itself, it is understood simultaneously that Consciousness has nowhere to go and nothing to become.

Therefore, from the point of view of ignorance, the search is the first step that Consciousness takes in the return to itself. From the point of view of Understanding, the search is the first step that Consciousness takes away from itself. In neither case does Consciousness ever go anywhere.

Even when Consciousness has veiled itself in a cloak of beliefs, doubts, fears and feelings, the taste of its own unlimited, free and fearless nature is embedded within every experience and this taste is often experienced as a sort of nostalgia or longing.

This longing is often wrongly associated with an event or a time in our lives, often in childhood, when things seemed to be better, when life seemed to be happier. However, this longing is not for a state that existed in the past – it is for the peace and freedom of Consciousness that lies behind and is buried within every current experience.

What was present 'then' as 'Happiness' was simply the unveiled presence of this very Consciousness that is seeing and understanding these words.

Consciousness projects this current experience out of itself. It then loses itself in this projection, in the mind/body/world that it has projected from within itself, and identifies itself with a part of it. It is as if it says to itself, "I am no longer this open, free, unlimited Consciousness. Rather I am this limited fragment that I have just created within myself. I am a body."

In doing so Consciousness forgets itself. It forgets its own unlimited nature. This forgetting is known as 'ignorance.' It is Consciousness *ignoring* itself.

As a result of this Self-forgetting, the nostalgia appears and Consciousness longs to return to itself, to be free. It does not realise, for the time being, that at every moment of this prodigal journey it is always only ever itself.

Meditation is simply the liberation of this projection from the burden of separation. It is the unwinding of the self-contraction, the unthreading of this web of confusion.

Instead of focusing its attention on the limited fragment, on the separate entity it has taken itself to be, Consciousness gives its own attention back to itself as it truly is. It returns to itself. It remembers itself.

And instead of projecting the world outside of itself, Consciousness reclaims it, takes it back inside itself.

41

The activity of identifying with a fragment and the activity of projecting the world outside, are one and the same activity. And by the same token, when one activity ceases, the other collapses.

Consciousness is so accustomed to thinking of itself as a limited entity and to the concomitant projection of the world outside of itself that it seems to begin with, that remembering itself, returning to itself, is a *counter* activity, something that Consciousness needs to *do* in order to find itself.

Like the opening of the hand, the unwinding of the self-contraction appears, to begin with, to be an activity.

However, each time Consciousness returns to itself, each time it relaxes its fixation on a separate entity, each time it opens itself without choice or preference to the full spectrum of whatever experience is appearing within itself, it is, without knowing it, undermining the habit of self-avoidance, the habit of avoiding its own Reality.

In this way, Consciousness becomes more and more accustomed to remaining in itself, as itself, to no longer pretending to be something else, something other than itself.

The impulse to contract into the separate entity is progressively undermined. Consciousness stays at home.

The impulses to search, to seek, to avoid, to pretend, to contract, keep appearing but Consciousness is no longer compelled by them. It recognises the impulses but no longer acts on them. And, as a result, the frequency and ferocity of these impulses begin to subside.

Consciousness no longer goes out of itself towards things. It stays at home within itself and things come to it. Things – that is, thoughts, feelings and perceptions – come to it, appear to it, arise within it, but Consciousness no longer needs to forget itself in order to experience the body, the mind and the world.

Consciousness shines in every experience.

There comes a moment where everything falls into place. This open, free, unlimited Consciousness that is our own intimate Self, realises that it has always been and will always be only itself, that it has never left itself for a fraction of a moment, that what appeared to be the return to itself, the remembering of itself, was simply the *recognition* of itself, the recognition that it has always, only ever been abiding in and as itself.

Consciousness realises that the separate entity that it previously took itself to *be*, is in fact simply an activity that it *does*, from time to time.

And by the same token, it realises that the activity that it seemed to *do* from time to time, the activity that we call meditation, is in fact what it always *is*.

It realises that meditation is not a state that comes and goes, but that it is that *in which* all states come and go.

Meditation is simply the natural presence of Consciousness, ever present, all-embracing, unchanging, unending, unlimited, Self-luminous, Self-knowing, Self-evident.

From the point of view of the limited, separate entity, all descriptions of meditation appear as something to be done by that separate entity. As soon as it is clearly seen that the separate entity is none other than a belief and a feeling that Consciousness entertains about itself, then the very words that previously seemed to describe a process or an activity called 'meditation,' that seemed to be an injunction to *do* something, are now understood to be simply a description of how things *are*.

From the point of view of ignorance, the 'person' is what we are and 'meditation' is something that we do from time to time. From the point of view of understanding, 'meditation' is what we are and the 'person' is something that we do from time to time.

Meditation is not something that we *do*. Whether we know it or not, it is what we *are*.

Ego

Ego means 'I,' and 'I' is Consciousness.

A jar gives a shape to the space inside it. However, when the jar is broken the space inside it remains exactly as it always was and is, neither inside nor outside.

In fact it is the space that enables the jar to have a shape, not the other way round.

The shape of the jar is just one of innumerable possibilities that are contained in potential within the space, including not having a shape at all.

What is commonly referred to as 'ego,' the separate entity, is the equivalent of the space, which is both inside and outside the jar, saying to itself, "I am the jar."

Ego is not an entity. It is an activity. It is an optional activity of identifying itself with a fragment that Consciousness is free to make or not, from moment to moment.

It is the activity of thinking and feeling that 'I,' this Consciousness that is seeing and understanding these words, am only this body/mind and not anything else that 'I' perceive.

This thought and feeling arises *within* Consciousness and is an *expression* of Consciousness. It is the activity of Consciousness *pretending* to be a body and a mind, and then *forgetting* that it is pretending and, instead, actually *thinking* and *feeling* that it *is* a body and a mind.

The ego, as it is commonly conceived, is simply this habit of pretending and forgetting, perpetuated through inadvertence.

It is the space inside and around the jar pretending that its essential nature has the features, the name and the shape of the jar.

It is Consciousness pretending that its essential nature has the same characteristics as the body/mind in which it seems to appear, and which in fact appears in it.

It is the gold in the earring telling itself that the name and shape of the earring is inherent in its own nature.

Consciousness' liberation from its identity with a fragment consists initially, in most cases, of returning to knowing itself as this open, welcoming, witnessing space of Presence.

However, it is not enough to simply know that 'I am Consciousness,' because this formulation leaves out everything that we do not consider to be 'I' – that is, others and the world. In other words, it leaves open the possibility that Consciousness is personal and limited.

Consciousness has to go further and rediscover its absolute identity with *all* things. It has to discover that 'I am everything,' that *this* Consciousness here is identical with *that* Reality out there. In other words it has to discover that it is impersonal and unlimited.

Even if the world out there is an illusion, that illusion is still *known*. It is *experienced*. The appearances that constitute our objective experience are changing all the time, but throughout the changing succession of appearances, *Knowing* or *Experiencing* is continuously present.

Knowing or Experiencing does not change with every changing appearance. Knowing or Experiencing does not flow with the flow of appearances. It is present and changeless throughout.

This *Knowingness*, this *Experiencingness*, that is present within every experience, *is* the light of Consciousness. It illumines every experience. This Knowingness is known as 'I.' It is our most intimate Self.

'I,' Identity, *is* Knowingness.

Knowingness is not what I *do*. It is what I *am*.

Knowingness goes into the make of every experience.

Therefore 'I' go into the make of every experience.

'I' *am* the Experiencing in every experience.

Likewise the world or an object *is* the experience of it. We have no evidence of a world that exists outside our experience of it. Nor is it ever possible to have such an experience, because experience itself is the touchstone of evidence.

If we separate Experiencing from an object, be that object a thought, a sensation or a perception, the object vanishes. However, Experiencing remains, experiencing itself.

Nothing exists outside our experience of it, as far as we know.

Therefore, if 'I' is *Experiencing* and if the world is made of our *Experiencing* of the world, then 'I' and the world, the object, are one.

The world as a separate and independent entity falls apart when we see this directly.

We have two names, 'I' and 'other,' for that which is in fact one thing. And we have one name, Oneness, for that which is in fact not a thing. It is nameless.

From the limited point of view of mind the Nameless is the unknowing of all things. From the point of view of Reality it is the Knowingness in the experience of all things.

Ego is a mode of functioning. It is an activity, not an entity. It is ignorant only in the sense that it occurs when Consciousness *ignores* itself.

We can still function very well in the apparent world of time and space without the sense of being a separate entity.

In fact free of the limited notions of being a separate entity, and the desires and fears that are required to maintain this position, life becomes free, alive and vibrant.

Experience is relieved of the demand to produce Happiness for a non-existent entity and flowers as a result.

Relationships are relieved of the demand to produce love and love shines in them naturally as a result.

And when there is no engagement with the body, mind or world, the default position of Consciousness is not to shrink back into the isolated cell of a self-contracted entity, not to collapse back into a person.

It is to remain as it is, transparent, luminous Presence, open, empty, silent and available, ready to take its shape as the totality of experience at every moment.

Imagine that you have spent your whole life living in a large house serving a demanding old man who lives in a room on the top floor.

Although you never see the man, you spend from morning till night doing his chores. One evening, during a rare break, you are lamenting your fate to a friend. The friend suggests that you reason with the old man.

When he hears that you never see him, let alone speak to him, he is puzzled and encourages you to go and find him.

To begin with you are reluctant but after several such encounters with your friend, you venture into the old man's room.

On your first visit you only have the courage to peep round the door but you cannot see the man. When you report this to your friend he encourages you to be bolder and have a good look in the room.

You make several visits to the old man's room and each time you search his quarters a little more thoroughly. It is only after several visits that you are convinced that there is no old man.

However, such are your habits that for some time you continue to wake at six every morning and perform many of the tasks that you used to perform while serving the imaginary old man. Some of these habits cease immediately, whilst others take time to come to an end.

In this story the old man is the separate entity and the friend is the teacher who encourages you to look inside and find out who this one that rules your life really is.

As we look more and more deeply into the nature of ourselves we find that there is no entity there. We spend our lives serving a non-existent entity. It is only our imagination that binds us and it is clarity that liberates.

In most cases this requires revisiting the issue many times, each time going a little more deeply into it, in order to be absolutely certain that there is no personal entity there.

Even after this discovery, some of the habits of the body/mind that were developed while serving the non-existent old man may linger out of inertia, but in time they will dwindle.

Our subservience to a separate entity consists, at the level of the mind, in the belief that 'I' am a separate, personal entity, and at the level of the body, as a feeling that 'I' am this body, or 'I' am *in* this body.

However, Consciousness is never actually bound by this belief or feeling. It just thinks and feels that it is. It pretends to bind itself by imagining itself as such, and therefore experiences itself as such.

However, as soon as it stops this pretence, it goes back to its natural state. As a result, the patterns of thinking, feeling and behaving that were allied to the pretence of separation, gradually unwind and are replaced more and more by thoughts, feelings and behaviours that are more in line with the natural state.

Consciousness Is Its Own Content

As a pedagogical tool, the Advaita or non-dual teaching sometimes refers to Consciousness and its contents, the appearances that arise within it, as two separate elements. This establishes the independence of Consciousness from appearances and the dependence of appearances on Consciousness.

As such it is a useful tool that uproots the conventional model of a Consciousness that is dependent on objects and of a world that exists separate and independent from Consciousness.

However, once this truth has been established, this formulation itself becomes a limitation and inhibits further understanding. What was true from the point of view of the conventional, dualistic paradigm, becomes untrue in the face of a deeper exploration into the nature of experience.

So let us look again at the formulation that objects appear within Consciousness, and that when they disappear, Consciousness remains without content.

In the analogy of the ocean, the waves are a metaphor for the appearances that arise upon or within the ocean of Consciousness.

The content of the waves is water, just as the content of an appearance is Consciousness.

The shape of the wave is the form that the water takes. It is the *form* of the appearance. 'Wave' is its name. But the *content* of that appearance is not wave. It is water.

Similarly, in order to 'appear,' Consciousness 'clothes' itself in name and form. It takes the shape of an appearance by projecting itself through mind and senses.

However, the *content* of every experience is Consciousness itself.

So objects – that is, thoughts, sensations and perceptions – are not the *content* of Consciousness. *Consciousness* alone is the content of Consciousness. Thoughts, sensations and perceptions are the names and forms that Consciousness takes in the process of manifestation.

When the waves die down, does their *content* disappear? No, the *appearance* of the waves ceases, but their *content*, the water, remains exactly as it always is.

Similarly the *content* of appearances is Consciousness and when the *appearance* disappears, their *content* does not. So the *content* of Consciousness *is* Consciousness itself. Consciousness is its own content. It never becomes anything else.

This can be reformulated in a way that is closer to our actual experience, by saying that the content of everything is Consciousness and this Consciousness is what we intimately know ourselves to be.

Consciousness is our own Reality and the Reality of all appearances.

In this way each formulation of Truth reveals the limitations of and replaces less complete formulations that precede it, and is then itself exposed and replaced by a formulation that is closer to direct experience.

As this exploration of the nature of experience deepens even the subtlest formulations are seen to be inadequate. The point at which they touch the experience to which they refer is precisely the point at which they collapse into the Silence that is their source.

One who is fearful of leaving his home projects all sorts of unpleasant things onto the outside world in order to justify his desire to remain indoors. Everything he sees and hears of the outside world seems to justify his attitude towards it and it will be very difficult to persuade such a person that it is in fact his attitude of fear that *causes* the world to appear in a certain way, rather than being the *result* of the way the world inherently is.

In the same way Consciousness becomes accustomed to thinking and feeling that it lives inside the body/mind and it substantiates this habit with layer upon layer of belief and feeling. Once it has taken this position, its experience seems to substantiate the truth of its beliefs and feelings.

However, such is the nature of Maya, the creative display of manifestation, that the opposite is also true: when Consciousness begins to relieve itself of its exclusive identification with a body/mind, it receives all sorts of confirmations from the world that it is on the right track.

The ego (Consciousness-pretending-to-be-a-separate-entity) is a past master at appropriating whatever is available in order to perpetuate itself, and for this purpose 'Truth' will suffice as well as anything else. In some ways it is the ultimate security because it cannot be trumped.

For instance, the ego uses the so-called understanding that 'Consciousness is all there is' and therefore 'anything is as good as anything else,' as an excuse to justify its activity of isolation.

However, the ego is a pretence, a pretence that Consciousness chooses to undertake out of its own freedom.

The attitude that Consciousness is all there is, is true if it comes from understanding, but it is not true if it comes from belief, from the ego. The ego is, by definition, the exclusive mixture of Consciousness with a body/mind, and therefore it cannot claim at the same time to be everything.

52

The *belief* that Consciousness is all there is does not put an end to the suffering which is inherent in Consciousness' exclusive identification with a single body/mind, and therefore the search, although temporarily subdued by this apparent attitude of tolerance and acceptance, will inevitably appear again at some stage.

It is disingenuous to say, "Everything is Consciousness, therefore I accept my suffering and negativity as an expression of that Consciousness and cannot, as a result, do anything about it."

Suffering is *already* a rejection of the current situation, a *lack* of acceptance of the current situation as it is. This rejection is the counterpart of Consciousness' exclusive identification with a body/mind. That is what suffering boils down to.

If our credo is, "Everything is Consciousness, therefore everything is as good as anything else, therefore I cannot and need not change my suffering," then why not apply that attitude to the current situation in the first place and welcome it exactly as it is? Instead of accepting our *rejection* of the current situation, why not simply accept the *current* situation itself? Suffering would cease right there.

This so-called acceptance of the rejection of the moment is not the true, impartial, benevolent welcoming of everything within Consciousness. It is fear dressed up as understanding, pseudo Advaita. As such it is the very activity of ego itself, perpetuating its own isolation and misery.

Ego is simply the exclusive mixture of impersonal Consciousness, which is seeing and understanding these words now, with a single body and mind.

It is an *activity* of Consciousness or, more accurately, the *shape* that this impersonal Consciousness takes from time to time.

Therefore the Peace and Happiness that are inherent in Consciousness are also inherent in the ego, in the alleged separate entity, in the same way that gold is inherent in the earring.

In fact we could say that ego was the *taste* of Peace and Happiness itself, mixed with the *belief* and *feeling* that Peace and Happiness are not present.

It is the earring saying to itself, "I long to sparkle with the beauty and brightness of gold," without realising that gold itself is already where its Existence, its Beauty comes from.

In the same way, every experience is only the presence of Consciousness shining.

We do not have to go anywhere else, or do anything else to know or experience this. It is all we ever experience.

Trying to go anywhere else or to see anything else in order to experience Presence, is precisely the denial of this very Presence shining here in this moment, *as* this moment. At the same time Consciousness shines in its very denial of itself, and in its subsequent search for itself.

To search for itself as an object is like the earring saying to itself, "I have to become something else, to do something else, in order to experience myself as gold." However, it is already, only gold. Whether it is turned into a bracelet or a necklace, it will always only ever be gold. The gold is not hidden behind and within the earring. It shines *as* the earring. The earring *is* its shining.

It is true that the name and the shape of the earring can attract our attention so strongly that we do not realise that we are looking at gold. We see only the name and shape of the earring. As soon as we see the gold we realise that when we are looking at the earring we are simultaneously looking at gold.

Just as in the conventional physical model of the world, we know that when we see objects we in fact see only light, so in Reality when we see the appearance of objects we know simultaneously that we in fact see only Consciousness.

That is, Consciousness, our Self, is only ever perceiving or experiencing itself.

From the point of view of mind, objects veil Consciousness. From the point of view of Reality, objects reveal Consciousness.

Imagine watching a football game on television. The drama is so exciting that all we see are the players, the pitch, the ball, etc At the end of the game we turn the television off and we see the screen.

At that moment we realise that we were in fact always seeing the screen, but the screen itself appeared to have taken the name and the shape of the players, the pitch and the ball.

The screen is in fact never obscured by the appearance of the game. It is all we ever see. We just sometimes fail to notice it. The players *seem* to obscure the screen but in fact they do not. Rather they *reveal* it. However, in doing so, they do not reveal something that is *hidden*. They reveal something, the screen, that is always in plain view, that is always being perceived, but is sometimes not noticed.

The screen is not *created* by turning off the television. It is *revealed* by it and, by the same token, revealed to have always been present.

When we turn the television on again, it becomes obvious that we are seeing the screen *and* the players simultaneously. The screen is the support and the substance of the players.

The screen is not hidden *behind* the players. While the players are present, the screen and the players are one and the same thing. We cannot separate them. They are identical.

We do not need to do anything special in order to understand that we see the screen and the players simultaneously. In fact once it is obvious, it becomes absurd to think that the screen and the players are separate or different from one another.

Having said that, turning off the television is necessary, in most cases, to draw attention to the presence of the screen, to show that the screen was there first, to show that the players depend on the screen but that the screen does not depend on the players.

Once this has become clear, we can turn the television back on again and not lose sight of this understanding.

Turning off the television is the equivalent of taking one's stand as the witness of all things. It puts the objects witnessed – that is, the mind, the body and the world – at a distance so to speak, and draws attention to the presence and primacy of Consciousness.

Once this becomes obvious we can look again at the full spectrum of objects that appear to the witness. We see now that Consciousness is not just their *support* but also their *substance*, in the same way that the screen is both the support and the substance of the players, the pitch and the ball.

In this way the witness is relieved of its last layer of limitation and objectivity and is revealed to be unlimited, impersonal Consciousness itself, *in* which and *as* which, rather than simply *to* which, all appearances appear.

Consciousness does not just *perceive* Reality. It *is* Reality.

We can still enjoy the match. We can still get excited or disappointed by the drama but, either way, we know and feel that it is only the screen.

It is only Presence that is dancing in this and every moment.

In the traditional Vedantic teachings the *veiling* power of appearances is sometimes emphasised and, because of this, appearances are sometimes considered to obscure the background of Consciousness.

In this tradition, 'Maya', appearance, is translated by the word 'illusion,' with a slightly negative connotation. However, it is not the appearance that is illusory. It is its apparent independence and separation from Consciousness that is illusory.

However, in the Tantric approach these very same appearances are understood to *reveal* and *express* the background itself, and therefore in this tradition, Maya is seen as a creative display of energies that derives from their source and thus leads back to it.

So precisely the same appearances can be said either to veil or reveal their source, depending on the level or point of view from which we look at them.

Knowingness Is The Substance Of All Things

The apparent continuity of any object is in fact the continuity of Consciousness. We could say that in the stream of experience it is 'Knowingness' or 'Experiencing' that persists, that is continuous, and that an appearance is simply a modulation of this Knowingness. An appearance has no substance or continuity of its own.

Knowingness is present before, during and after every experience.

During any appearance itself, Knowingness takes the shape of that appearance. During the absence of any appearance, it simply remains as it always is.

As an *appearance* every object is limited. For instance, the body/ mind is limited as an appearance. But in Reality, the *substance* of this appearance is Consciousness itself and as such has no limitations.

From the point of view of ignorance, Consciousness seems to take on the qualities of the body/mind. That is, it seems to become personal and limited.

From the point of view of understanding, our true body and our true mind is impersonal, unlimited Consciousness itself.

Before and after every appearance, Knowingness simply knows itself *as* itself. This Self-knowing is colourless, transparent, Self-luminous and Self-evident.

Whatever remains after the disappearance of an object has no objective qualities. However, 'Experiencingness' remains. That is what Consciousness is. It is pure Experiencing.

When there are no objects present, this Experiencingness remains as it always is, experiencing itself.

Experiencingness or Knowingness are synonyms for Consciousness.

The desire to experience 'Experiencingness' or to know 'Knowingness' as an object, is the very thing that prevents us from abiding knowingly *as* 'Experiencingness' or 'Knowingness.' By seeking for itself elsewhere, in this way, Consciousness overlooks itself.

It is this agitation, the desire to experience Consciousness as an object, which seems to veil the experience of Consciousness knowing itself.

In spite of this, Consciousness is in fact *always* knowing itself. It cannot 'not know' itself, because *knowing* is its nature. However, it sometimes knows itself without knowing that it knows, without recognising itself. It is not aware that it is aware of itself.

The desire to experience Consciousness as an object comes from the belief that Consciousness is not already present. This belief is fuelled and substantiated by a deep sense of lack at the level of the body, the feeling, "I want something. I need something."

Every time this sense of lack is relieved by the acquisition of a desired object, Consciousness briefly glimpses itself, and this experience is known as Happiness. In fact it is not a *brief* moment. It is a *timeless* moment.

However, it is not the acquired object that causes the Happiness. It is the dissolution of the sense of lack, which is apparently brought about by the acquisition of the object, which allows the *pre-existing* Happiness to be revealed.

So the relaxation of this desire to experience Consciousness an object, which actually prevents us from abiding as Consciousness knowingly, requires more than simply the understanding that Consciousness is not an object.

It requires a deep sensitivity to the sense of lack, to the feeling that we need something that is not present in order to make us happy, to the feelings and impulses at the level of the body and how we escape them through thinking.

Once this is understood, we no longer need the acquisition of an object to dissolve the sense of lack. We go directly to the sense of lack itself and face it as it is. We do not act on the impulse and escape it through thinking, desiring and acting. We have the courage to face it. We have the courage not to try and relieve it, not to do anything about it.

We simply allow the feeling of lack to be fully present. We do not add anything to it. That is easy because we, Consciousness, are already the allowing or welcoming of all things.

We simply let Consciousness take care of everything.

The clear seeing of these feelings reveals that they are in fact no more than neutral bodily sensations with no inherent power to generate thinking, desiring or fearing, let alone a sense of lack or separation.

This downgrading of feelings to bodily sensations in our under-standing, is accomplished effortlessly through clear seeing.

We do not *do* anything to the feelings. In fact we *stop* doing some-thing to them. We stop investing them with the power to veil Real-ity. We stop investing them with the power to generate unhappiness and its attendant seeking.

As soon as we stop superimposing feelings onto bodily sensations, they cease to be an abode of ignorance and confusion, and are revealed instead as a beautiful display of creative energies dancing in the emptiness of Presence, revealing its fullness moment by moment.

Of course, desires continue to arise, but their purpose is no longer the *avoidance* of feeling nor the *attainment* of Happiness. Their purpose is to *express* Happiness. Their purpose – in fact their *nature* – is to manifest, share and celebrate Happiness.

Our True Body

Experience always takes place *now*, in the present, so if we want to explore the nature of Reality, all we have is this current experience.

In this current experience we have all the information that is needed to understand the nature of ourselves and of Reality, because both we, whatever we are, and Reality, whatever it is, are present.

All that is necessary is to stick very closely to our actual experience and not rely on concepts or ideas from the past about the way we think things are. We have to come very cleanly to this exploration of experience and only permit that which we know for ourselves to be true.

In this moment there is *something* that is being experienced. We may not know *what* that something is. For instance, it may be a dream or a hallucination, but we know that there is *something*.

There is *something* that is known – that is, the body, mind and world – and there is *something* – that which we refer to as 'I' – that is experiencing or knowing the known.

These two, these apparent two, the experienced and the Experiencer, the known and the Knower, the perceived and the Perceiver, are in fact always one seamless totality. They are not two things in our actual experience.

However, we tend to focus mainly, if not exclusively, on the objective aspect of this seamless totality. In most cases our attention is primarily occupied with thoughts and images, feelings and sensations, and sense perceptions – that is, with the mind, the body and the world.

By contrast, in these contemplations we focus on the subjective aspect of experience rather than the objective aspect. We give our attention to the Perceiver rather than the perceived.

In spite of the fact that experience is always one seamless totality, we artificially separate the Perceiver from the perceived, the Experiencer from the experienced, the subjective aspect of experience from the objective aspect.

The purpose of doing this is to draw attention to the subjective aspect, to the Knower, the Perceiver, the Experiencer, to the presence of Consciousness, which witnesses whatever it is that is being experienced from moment to moment.

Normally we are so absorbed in the objective aspect of experience that we overlook the presence of Consciousness within and behind every experience.

Consciousness, or that to which we refer as 'I,' is that which *perceives* or *experiences*. It is that which witnesses the mind, the body and the world. It is that which is seeing and understanding these words right now.

In this moment something is being experienced and whatever that something is, whether it is the mind, the body or the world, it is being perceived or experienced *by* Consciousness, by that which we call 'I,' or 'me.'

This Consciousness is an undeniable fact of our experience. Even the denial of Consciousness requires Consciousness.

However, we have forgotten that the real nature of this 'I,' of our Self, is Consciousness, the Presence that is witnessing and experiencing whatever it is that is being experienced in this moment.

This presence of Consciousness stands alone, independent of any of the objects of the mind, body and world that appear to it, in the same way that a mirror stands alone, independent of whatever is reflected within it.

However, we have confused and identified this witnessing Consciousness with the body and the mind and, as a result, we have come to think and feel that 'I' is *something*, that it is a body/mind.

The body, mind and world are all equally *objects* of Consciousness. However, having mistakenly identified Consciousness with the body/mind, we have transferred the status of subject, which properly belongs to Consciousness alone, onto the body/mind.

In this way we have come to think and feel that it is 'I' as the body/mind, which experiences the world.

However, the body/mind does not witness or experience anything. It is itself witnessed, experienced.

We experience the mind (thoughts and images) and the body (sensations) in just the same way that we experience the world (sense perceptions).

Each of these experiences is equally an *object* of Consciousness. The mind and the body are no less objects of Consciousness than is the world.

In this way we return the mind and the body, in our understanding, to their proper place as *objects* of Consciousness, along with the world.

And by giving the mind and the body back to the objective realm, we are, by the same token, returning the 'I,' in our understanding, to Consciousness.

In our contemplation we give attention to this witnessing Consciousness.

All that means is that we abide as this witnessing Consciousness *knowingly*. That is, this Consciousness abides in itself, as itself, knowingly.

We allow the mind, the body and the world to appear, to remain and to disappear in this presence of Consciousness. That is what they are doing anyway, so we simply cooperate with what is always already the case.

In this state we know our Self, Consciousness, to be nothing that is conceivable or perceivable, and yet we know that we *are*.

So, having mistakenly identified 'I,' Consciousness, with the body/mind and come, as a result, to know our Self as *something*, we now come to understand our Self as the witness, as nothing objective.

Consciousness, 'I,' the subject, is already at rest. It is already peaceful. In fact it is Peace itself.

Peace is inherent in Consciousness.

The agitation of the mind, the body and the world appear in Consciousness, but Consciousness is not agitated by them.

It is our experience that Consciousness, that which we know our Self to be, is always present, always remains as it is, unchanging and unmoving, and always impartially welcomes into itself the totality of our objective experience, irrespective of the nature of that experience.

Taking our stand as this ever-present Consciousness, we can look again at our experience and see that we never actually experience the mind, the body or the world in the way that we usually conceive them.

The mind consists of this current thought or image, whatever it is we are thinking or imagining in this moment. There is no container called the mind in which all our memories, hopes, fears and desires etc are stored. Whenever a memory, hope, fear or desire etc appears, it appears as a current thought.

The idea that there is a mind which contains memories, hopes, fears and desires, is itself simply a thought that appears from time to time like any other thought, in Consciousness.

There is no mind as such. The existence of a mind is simply an idea, a concept. It is a useful concept but it is not a fact of experience.

Likewise we do not experience the body in the way we normally conceive it. In fact there is no body as such. There is a series of sensations and perceptions appearing in Consciousness. And from time to time there is a thought or an image of a 'body,' which is considered to be the sum total of all these sensations and perceptions.

However this thought or image appears in Consciousness in exactly the same way as the sensations and perceptions to which it apparently refers. And this apparent body is made of the same substance as a thought. It is made of mind, taking mind in the broadest sense of the term, to include sensing and perceiving as well as thinking.

If we stick closely to the actual experience of our bodily sensations, we see that they are shapeless and contourless. We may experience a visual perception of the skin and from several different perceptions conceive a well-defined border which contains all other bodily sensations. However, this conception does not describe the Reality of our experience.

The visual perception of the surface of the body is one perception. A bodily sensation is another perception. When one of these perceptions is present the other is not. If they are both present, they are one perception, one experience.

One perception cannot appear within another. All perceptions appear within Consciousness. We do not experience a sensation *inside* the body. What we call the body is in fact the experience of a sensation.

We do not experience a sensation *within* a well-defined contour of skin. We experience a sensation *within* Consciousness and we experience a visual perception *within* Consciousness.

We can explore this further by imagining what it would be like to draw our actual experience of the body at any given moment, on a piece of paper. Would it look anything like the body we normally conceive? Would it not be a collection of minute, amorphous abstract marks, floating on the page, without a shape or a border?

Is not the actual *experience* of the body a collection of minute, amorphous, tingling sensations free-floating in the space of Consciousness?

And if we look at these sensations, are they not permeated and saturated with the presence of Consciousness in which they appear?

The continuity and coherence that we normally ascribe to the body, in fact belong to Consciousness.

In fact our true body *is* Consciousness. It is Consciousness that houses all the sensations that we normally refer to as 'the body.'

Our true body is open, transparent, weightless and limitless. It is inherently empty and yet contains all things within itself. That is why such an empty body is also inherently loving.

It is the welcoming embrace of all things.

'I' Am Everything

In order to draw attention to the presence and primacy of this witnessing Consciousness, we can divide the seamless totality of our experience into a perceiving subject, Consciousness, and a perceived object, the body, mind and world.

As we have seen, this enables us to explore the experience of Consciousness and to see if there is any validity to the claim that it is limited to an individual, personal body/mind.

It also enables us to explore the nature of the object. What is an object really made of?

What is the relationship between the mind, body and world that appear within Consciousness, and Consciousness itself?

For instance, take a sound that is present now. Do we experience a boundary between that sound and the Consciousness that perceives it? Is there a border between them?

The perception of a sound, the sensation that we call 'my hand' and the current thought, all appear free-floating in the same space of Consciousness. Is that not our actual experience?

Is it true that our thoughts are on the inside of this Consciousness and that sounds are on the outside?

What is our actual experience of the boundary between what is 'inside' myself and what is 'outside' myself? There is no experience of such a boundary!

If we think that we do experience such a boundary, is not that boundary itself a perception, an object that is free-floating in Consciousness, along with whatever else is being experienced in the moment?

Does this apparent border really separate the thought 'inside' myself from the sound 'outside'?

Is it true that the sensation that we call our hand, for instance, is closer to us – that is, closer to this witnessing Consciousness – than the sound we are hearing in the distance?

'In the distance' is a concept. The sound appears *here*, in me, in Consciousness, in exactly the same place as the sensation we call our hand.

Do they not both appear at an equal distance from Consciousness, which is no distance at all?

Are they not both equally one with Consciousness, with 'I,' with that which experiences them?

And 'I,' Consciousness, am *here*. I am always *here*.

This *here* is not a place. It is absolute intimacy, absolute immediacy, absolute identity.

Why do we think that the sensation we call our hand is closer to us than the sound 'in the distance'? Is that our actual experience?

If Consciousness is likened to the space in this room and the mind, the body and the world are likened to the objects that appear within it, is it true to say that the chair, for instance, that we are sitting on, is closer to the space in this room than the table? Is the floor closer to the space than the ceiling? That is absurd!

And yet when we say that our hand is closer to us, to Consciousness, than 'the sound in the distance,' or that a thought is closer to us than our hand, it is equally absurd. That is not our experience. Our experience is that each appears at the same zero distance from Consciousness.

And if we now look very closely at the *substance* of the object that is appearing within Consciousness, we find that it cannot be differentiated from it in any way. There is no part of the experience of an object that is not utterly saturated and permeated by Consciousness itself.

Consciousness is not simply the *witness* but also the *substance* of every object that appears within it.

Every object is *made* out of Consciousness. It is an *expression* of Consciousness.

To begin with we understand objects as appearing *to* Consciousness.

Then we understand that they appear *in* Consciousness.

Then we understand that they appear *as* Consciousness.

In this way Consciousness reabsorbs the body, the mind and the world into itself.

Even that formulation is not quite right, because it suggests that an object has somehow come from outside and has appeared *within* Consciousness, that Consciousness takes the object into itself.

However, Consciousness is there first, before the appearance of any object. The very first experience we ever had as a newborn infant was experienced *by* this very Consciousness that is present now, seeing these words.

Of course, it does not make sense to say 'before,' because when there are no objects there is no time, but we have to accept this limitation of language.

It is not that Consciousness takes the object into itself. It is that Consciousness *takes the shape* of the apparent object, through the faculties of sensing and perceiving, and yet at the same time always remains itself.

Initially Consciousness identifies itself with the object and in doing so it seems to forget itself. Later on, it takes the shape of the object without forgetting itself.

When Consciousness seems to forget itself, the 'object' is experienced as an object with its own apparent separate existence. When Consciousness takes the shape of the object *without* forgetting itself, the 'object' is experienced as an expression of Presence itself.

In fact Consciousness takes the shape of every experience we have. In this condition we, Consciousness, know ourselves to be *everything*.

The transparent, luminous, empty, Self-knowing nothingness, no-thing-ness, of Consciousness takes the shape of the totality of our experience. It knows itself as everything.

Consciousness is always only itself and yet, in exclusively identifying itself with an object, the body/mind, it *seems* to become *something*. It *seems* to become an object.

In disidentifying itself from the object, it realises itself as the subject. It realises itself as nothing, as empty. That is, it realises that it is not an object, not a 'thing.'

As it reconsiders the object from the position of the subject, it realises that the subject – that is, *itself* – goes into the make of the object. It realises itself as *everything*.

This condition could be called Love. It is the natural state in which the nothingness of the witness is liberated from any objectivity or limitation and realises itself to be the very substance of everything. Consciousness knows itself as *everything*.

It realises that everything is included within itself and is an expression of itself.

It goes beyond subject and object. Subject and object collapse into that which is behind, beyond and within both. We could call this Being.

Consciousness becomes something, then nothing, then everything, and yet always remains itself.

Consciousness is known as the perceived, then the perceiver, then the perceiving, and yet throughout this process, Consciousness remains always only itself.

Consciousness never *goes* anywhere. Consciousness never *becomes* anything.

There is only Consciousness, there is only Being, which simultaneously creates, witnesses, expresses and experiences itself in every experience we have.

What We *Are*, It Is

The fact that there is experience tells us two things.

It tells us that there is Consciousness, that whatever it is that is conscious, is present and aware, that it is witnessing or experiencing whatever it is that is being experienced.

We refer to this Consciousness as 'I,' as 'me.' It is the subjective element in every experience. We do not know *what* that Consciousness is, but we know *that* it is.

What we are conscious *of*, does not tell us anything about the nature of Consciousness, other than that it is conscious and present, that it *is*. We know that it is *present*, that it has Being.

The fact that there is experience also tells us that there is *something* that is being experienced, that *something* is present. This *something* is the objective element in every experience. It is everything that is not 'me,' not 'I,' not Consciousness. We refer to it as 'that' or 'it.'

We may not know *what* this 'something' is, yet there is no doubt that *something* is being experienced.

It may be an illusion, a dream or a hallucination, and yet still it is *something*. It has Existence. It has Being. It has Reality.

What has been stated so far could be formulated simply as, 'I', the subject, experiences 'it' or 'that,' the object. It is the common view of experience.

What is not so common is to see clearly that we do not in fact know what anything truly is. We do not know the real nature of experience. We know nothing objective for certain.

In fact the mind, by definition, can *never* know the true nature of experience. However, it is not necessary to *know* the true nature of experience because, if we make a deep exploration of our experience, we discover that what we fundamentally *are*, *is* the true nature, the Reality of all that is perceived.

What we *are*, it *is*.

However, this identity of our Self with the Reality of all things is not an objective knowing.

In this unknowing, simply the fact that there is *something*, that there is Being, that there is Consciousness, is the most extraordinary thing.

In the light of this, walking on water or teleporting through space is no more remarkable than a speck of dust or the fly that has just landed on this table.

That the presence of Consciousness and Being are known as one, in the knowing of the speck of dust, makes the speck of dust the most extraordinary miracle.

It is for this reason that the Kashmiri Shaivites called this exploration of experience a yoga of 'wonder, astonishment and delight.'

We simply stand open, empty, silent, unknowing and wondrous.

Of course, into this openness, formulations arise that are appropriate responses to the current situation. They come from the situation itself and as a result they are hand-in-glove with it.

One example of such a response may be a formulation about the nature of Reality. This formulation will be a provisional response to a question or a situation. However, when the situation vanishes, the response vanishes with it.

The response never frames Reality, although it is an expression of it and points towards it.

The response arises from this Unknowingness, dances with the question for a while and then merges with it, returning it to its source, Silence.

In fact the real response is Silence itself. It is Silence that consumes the question.

If we take the subjective aspect of experience first, we see that it is impossible to know anything objective about it, about 'I,' about Consciousness. The simple reason for this is that anything that is known is by definition an object.

Anything we think we know about the subject is immediately transferred to the status of 'object.' It becomes the known, not the Knower.

Normally we identify this knowing 'I' or Consciousness with the mind and the body. We think that the mind and the body are 'me,' 'I,' the subject, and that everything else is 'the world,' 'that,' 'it,' the 'object.'

There is already a lack of clarity in this view, because the mind and the body are *known*. They are not the *Knower*. They cannot, therefore, be what we refer to as, 'I.'

It is clear from this that 'I,' Consciousness, although undeniably present, cannot be known as an object. It is the *Knower* of whatever is *known*.

However, Consciousness also knows *itself* because *knowing* is its nature. It is always present and therefore it always knows itself.

To *know* itself in this sense, is to *be* itself. Its being itself *is* its knowing itself.

Knowing and Being are identical when referring to Consciousness.

Turning now to the objective aspect of experience, the mind and the senses are the instruments through which whatever is experienced, is known. They are the instruments of perception.

We do not know *what* it is that is being experienced, but whatever it is, is experienced through the faculties of the mind and the senses.

Therefore, if we are to discover the real nature of the 'known,' the Reality of the 'world,' independent of the instruments through which they are known, we must divest the known of the qualities that are imparted by the instruments of perception.

That which is imparted by the mind is the name, the concept of what an object is. From the seamless totality of experience, we abstract an object and call it, say, 'a chair.'

That which is imparted by the senses is form – that is, shape, colour, touch, taste, smell, sound. If these faculties were different, the world would appear differently. We substantiate the abstraction that we have labelled 'chair' with qualities of sensation such as 'hard' or 'red.'

We clothe Reality in name and form.

What are the qualities of the known that are independent of the instruments through which they are known?

What remains of the known when the faculties *through which* it is known are removed? The *Existence* or *Reality* of the known, remains. That is, whatever it is that belongs to the known, that does not belong to mind or senses, remains.

Everything apart from the Existence or Being or Reality of an object is removed with the removal of the instruments of perception, with the removal of mind.

Anything objective that can be said about this Reality belongs to the realm of mind or senses, to that *through* which Reality is manifest, and so cannot be inherent in it.

However, we can say that Reality *exists*, that it *is*, that it has *Being*.

So we are left with the understanding that, when experience is divested of name and form, when experience is divested of the individual faculties through which it is perceived or apprehended, only the presence of Consciousness and Existence remains.

What is the relationship between Consciousness and Existence?

Both Consciousness and Existence are present in every experience and yet neither have objective qualities.

If they were different from one another, they would have to have defining qualities that distinguished and separated them.

We have already seen that all such defining qualities belong to the realm of the mind or senses, to the faculties of knowing, sensing and perceiving, and are therefore not inherent in Consciousness or Existence.

Therefore, if Consciousness and Existence are both present in every experience and yet neither of them have any qualities, they cannot be separate.

Consciousness and Existence are one and the same. That is our moment by moment experience.

We started with a model of experience that seemed to support the idea of a subject knowing an object through the medium of mind and senses. When the cloak or veil of mind and senses, of name and form, is removed, we are left with Consciousness and Existence.

When we look at our experience of Consciousness and Existence we find that they are identical.

This may seem like an abstract and complex line of reasoning that bears little relation to our day to day experience, but this realisation of the identity of Consciousness and Existence is in fact a very common and familiar experience.

It is known as Happiness or Peace.

We could say that when the knowing of any object is relieved of its objective qualities, the identity of Consciousness and Existence is revealed. This revelation is known as Happiness in relation to the body, Peace in relation to the mind and Beauty in relation to the world.

It is the mind and the senses that seem to separate the oneness of Consciousness/Existence into two parts, into 'me' and 'other,' this and that, subject and object.

The mind and the senses are like a prism through which the oneness of Consciousness/Existence appears to be refracted into 'ten thousand things.'

It is because of this veiling power of mind and senses that some spiritual traditions have shunned the body and the world, seeing them as a dangerous realm of illusion that distracts attention from the oneness of Consciousness/Existence.

However, although there is a place in the unfolding of understanding for this interpretation of mind and senses, because such a view enables us to stand back from their veiling power, it ultimately keeps the body and the world at a distance and therefore perpetuates the illusion of duality.

In fact the mind and senses do not actually divide Consciousness from Existence. They only appear to do so.

There is nothing illusory about the world. It is the separation between the Existence of the world and the presence of Consciousness, that is illusory. This illusion of a separate and independent Existence is created through mind and senses.

It is the creativity of Consciousness, through the faculties of mind and senses, which refracts Oneness into a dance of apparent multiplicity.

Time is the first language of the mind. Space is the first language of the senses. Remove time and space from experience – that is, remove name and form – and we are left with the oneness of Consciousness/ Existence. We are left with timeless, spaceless Presence, with Being.

Being shines in the self as Consciousness and in the world as Existence.

However, mind and senses are not imposed from the outside onto the oneness of Consciousness/Existence. They proceed from within it.

If we explore the actual experience of mind and senses, we find that their very substance is the Consciousness/Existence from which they proceed.

We could say that Consciousness/Existence gives birth to mind and senses, which give birth to time and space, which in turn give birth to the world, to 'ten thousand things.'

We could say that Consciousness/Existence takes a prodigal journey, *apparently* out of its own kingdom, into the realm of mind and matter. It is as though the seamlessness of Consciousness/Existence unfolds itself to become the world and then folds itself back up again, folds the world back into itself.

We experience this every time we make the transition from deep sleep to the dreaming state and from the dream state to the waking state.

At first mind is created within the timeless, unity of deep sleep, in which Oneness abides in its own unmanifest condition and in which everything is enfolded in potential.

We could say that this Oneness of deep sleep metamorphoses into mind, takes the shape of mind. This creates the world of dreams, of subtle images, in which time but not space, is present.

Then the Oneness of deep sleep creates within itself or *becomes* the faculties of sensing and perceiving, without ever becoming anything other than itself, and, as a result, space is created.

With the appearance of this new dimension, the waking state appears and with it the world.

At no time in this process is there an entity that wakes up, that proceeds from deep sleep to the dream state, or from the dream state to the waking state.

It is rather that the Oneness of deep sleep grows within itself, conceives and gives birth within itself, to the dreaming and waking worlds, which *appear* to proceed out of the womb of Presence, but in fact always remain *within* it.

That which is present in deep sleep, or rather that which *is* deep sleep, remains as the background and substance of the dreaming and waking states.

As soon as this is seen clearly to be the fact of our experience, the veiling power of mind and senses is transformed into a revealing power.

The mind and senses are double agents. They work for both ignorance and understanding.

This realisation is the moment the prodigal son turns around and proceeds back towards the father on exactly the same path that he originally took on his flight away from him.

This is also the moment at which the traditional spiritual path of renunciation becomes the tantric path of embrace and inclusion. It is the moment at which the full spectrum of experience is welcomed, explored and celebrated for what it truly is.

It is the transition from,"I am nothing" to "I am everything," from the path of discrimination to the path of Love.

It is the moment when the emptiness of Consciousness recognises itself as the fullness of experience.

It is the moment at which Consciousness recognises that it projects the world *within* itself, rather than *from* or *out of* itself.

We no longer feel that we are an entity located here and now, in the sense of being *inside* the body at a particular *moment* of time. Rather we come to understand the 'now' as timeless Presence, not a moment in time, and the 'here' as placeless Presence, not a location in space.

The mind, the body and the world are understood to be *expressions* of Consciousness rather than *distractions* from it.

The identity of 'I' and 'that' is realised. They do not unite. They have always been united. In fact they are not even united for they were never two things to begin with. Only now their unity is recognised. It recognises itself.

Peace And Happiness Are Inherent In Consciousness

The mind, body and the world appear to Consciousness, to 'me,' to 'I.' They are objects and Consciousness is their subject, that which experiences them.

Consciousness, that which we call 'I,' is always present in every experience and does not disappear between experiences.

Have we ever had the experience of our Self, Consciousness, disappearing? That is not possible. There would have to be something present to witness that disappearance, and that something would have to be conscious. It would in turn be that which we call 'I,' Consciousness.

When an object appears within this conscious Presence, this Presence knows itself as the witness of that object.

In deep sleep, 'I,' this conscious witnessing Presence, remains exactly as it always is in the waking and dreaming states.

There are no objects present in deep sleep and therefore there is no memory of that state. On waking, the mind interprets that state as a blank, a nothing, a void. However, an absence of memory is not a proof of non-existence.

On falling asleep the well organised images, sensations and perceptions of the waking state are gradually replaced by the less well organised images of the dreaming state but, during this transition, there is no experience of a change in the presence of Consciousness.

Likewise, as images fade from the dream state, Consciousness remains as it is, and this presence of Consciousness without objects is referred to as deep sleep.

At no stage in the transition from the waking state to deep sleep does Consciousness ever experience a change in its own presence or continuity.

Just as Consciousness remains completely unaffected by the changing flow of experience during the waking state, so Consciousness remains exactly the same during the transition from the waking state to the dreaming state, during the dreaming state itself, and during the transition from the dreaming state to deep sleep.

In fact the three states of waking, dreaming and deep sleep are misnamed. These three categories are based on the assumption that there is an entity, called 'I,' which makes the transition through these three states. Once it is clearly seen that there is no individual entity, it is seen, by the same token, that there are not three states.

A state is something that lasts for a certain period of time. It comes and goes. It would be more accurate to say that there is one condition, one ever-present condition, which we call 'I,' Consciousness, Presence, in which all apparent states come and go.

The apparent states of waking and dreaming are modulations of this one Presence.

Deep sleep is in fact simply the presence of Consciousness shining by itself. That is why it is so peaceful and enjoyable!

It only becomes a state, *appears* to become a state, when it is mistakenly conceived of by the mind to have lasted for a certain length of time. However, there is no time in deep sleep.

These three states are not well-defined categories. It would be more accurate to say that there is a flow of objects, gross and subtle, that takes place within this ever-present Consciousness.

During the waking state the objects seem dense, coherent and closely packed together. There is not much space between them. As the dream state begins, the objects become lighter and more loosely held together. There is more space between them. In deep sleep there are no objects. There is empty space.

That empty space is the presence of the background, the presence of Consciousness, 'I.' It is referred to as being empty only from the mind's point of view, because there is nothing objective there. However, from its *own* point of view, it is experienced as fullness, as Presence, Self-luminous, Self-knowing and Self-evident.

It is the same space that is present during the intervals between objects in the dreaming and waking states. It is also the same space of Consciousness that is present during the *appearance* of objects in the waking and dreaming states.

In the dreaming and waking states, the emptiness of Consciousness seems to be coloured by the appearance of objects. However, Consciousness is not coloured by anything outside itself.

Consciousness itself takes the shape of every appearance although it is itself shapeless, just as water takes the shape of a wave, although it is itself shapeless.

This Consciousness that is present during the appearance of the subtle object we call a thought, is exactly the same Consciousness that is present during the appearance of the subtle object we call the dream.

Likewise, the Consciousness that is present during the appearance of the gross object we call the world, is also the same Consciousness that is present during the appearance of the dream.

In this respect the world is a form of thought. The world is made of perceptions. These perceptions are made out of perceiving. They are made out of mind, out of the same substance that a thought is made of.

A thought, a sensation, a perception and a dream are all made out of the same 'stuff' and they all appear in the same space. They are made out of and appear within the same Consciousness, and it is this same Consciousness that is present during the gaps between appearances and during objectless deep sleep.

As the object changes or leaves, either during each state or during the transition between states, the Consciousness that is present *behind* the object as its witness and *within* the object as its substance, remains exactly as it always is, ever-present and unchanged. Any changes that are experienced in the body, mind or world are changes that appear *to* this Consciousness.

Consciousness itself is not changed by the images that appear *to* it or *within* it any more than a mirror is changed by the changing images that are reflected in it.

In fact Consciousness not only is present as the continuous, unchanging *witness* of objects, but it also *expresses* itself simultaneously *as* objects. It is the *substance* of objects.

However, although objects are made out of Consciousness, this Consciousness does not change as the objects change, any more than water changes when waves change.

Consciousness knows itself all the time. How could something whose nature is Knowingness not know itself all the time?

How could something whose nature is Consciousness not be conscious of itself all the time?

There are no objects present in deep sleep, therefore there is no memory of it. And yet on waking up, something lingers, something is left over. The saying, 'I slept well,' refers to an experience. It refers to the experience of Peace that was present during deep and undisturbed sleep.

The saying, 'I slept badly,' refers to some sort of disturbance, that is, to some sort of object. Either we mean that we woke up in the night and remained awake while wanting to be asleep, in this case the term 'sleeping badly' actually refers to the waking state, not the deep sleep state. Or we mean that we had disturbing dreams that kept us from the Peace of deep sleep, and in this case the term 'sleeping badly' refers to the dream state.

In neither case is the experience of deep sleep itself referred to as a bad experience. In fact when we say that we slept badly it is always to the *absence* of deep sleep that we refer.

There are, by definition, no objects present in deep sleep and for that reason it is peaceful there. And because deep sleep and Peace always coexist, it can be said that Peace is *inherent* in deep sleep. It is not even true to say that Peace is inherent in deep sleep, because we do not experience two things there. Rather deep sleep *is* Peace.

Therefore, if Peace is identical to deep sleep and, as we have seen, deep sleep *is* the presence of Consciousness without objectivity, it follows that Peace is *inherent* in Consciousness, that Peace and Consciousness are one.

We acknowledge this experience every time we say that we have slept well. That statement comes from an experience.

There are no objects present in deep sleep and therefore Peace cannot be dependent on objects. This in turn implies that Peace is independent of any of the states or conditions of the body, mind or world.

Consciousness is always present, not only in deep sleep but in the dreaming and waking states as well. As Peace is inherent in Consciousness, Peace must also be present at all times, under all conditions and in all states.

It does not make sense to talk about the presence of Consciousness 'at all times,' because Consciousness does not exist in time. Time exists as an idea in Consciousness. However, we have to accept these limitations of language if we are to speak of Presence.

If Peace is independent of all conditions of the body, mind and world, it implies that Peace is not a state, that it does not come and go. It is present behind and within *all* appearances of the body, mind and world.

For this reason Peace cannot be the result of any activity in the body, mind or world. It cannot be the outcome of a practice. It cannot be created, maintained or lost. It always *is*.

In fact we can go further than that and say that just as everything is ultimately an expression of Consciousness, so ultimately is everything an expression of Peace.

Every experience is the shape of Silence.

From the experience of deep sleep it is clear that Peace is inherent in Consciousness, that it is not an attribute of objects, situations, circumstances or events.

However, there are other occasions in the waking state when the experience of Consciousness without an object is also present. For instance, there are many moments in the waking state between one perception and the next when Consciousness stands alone, without an object.

These gaps or intervals are experiences in the sense that Consciousness is always experiencing itself, whether or not objects are present, but they have no objective content.

Of course, it does not make sense to assign these intervals a duration in time. Time is the distance between two events and during these intervals there are no objects and therefore no events. If no objects are present there, no time is present there.

This timeless non-experience cannot be remembered, in the same way that deep sleep cannot be remembered. No memory of this interval appears in Consciousness, because there was nothing present there apart from the transparent objectless presence of Consciousness itself.

In that sense these intervals are non-experiences. However, it would be incorrect to say that there was no experience during these moments. There is no *objective* experience and yet Consciousness is present 'there' experiencing itself.

Consciousness is the witness and substance of every objective experience, and when no object is present, such as in the interval between perceptions, Consciousness remains as it always is, knowing itself. This objectless Self-knowing is the *substance* of these intervals.

So experience does not stop when the object vanishes, only the *objective* aspect of experience, the name and form, ceases. Experience itself, experiencing itself, continues.

Once we see clearly that it is only Consciousness that is experienced during the waking and dreaming states, by the same token, it becomes clear that when no objects are present, the same experience of Consciousness experiencing itself simply continues. In fact, nothing else has ever happened, other than this experience of Consciousness knowing itself.

These intervals are ever-present and timeless, just as the blue sky, which seems to be present only in the gaps between clouds, is in fact present behind as well as within the clouds themselves.

These intervals are the timeless background of Consciousness, in which objects, including the concept of time, appear from time to time. The sense of duration that is suggested by the term 'interval' is due to the limitation of language only, and should not be interpreted as implying that these intervals last in time.

The experiences of Understanding, Love and Beauty are all experiences of this timeless, objectless Self-knowing, Self-recognition.

During these timeless intervals Consciousness is simply present, as it is in deep sleep. It knows itself directly.

After this timeless interval, Consciousness takes the shape of the next appearance and may identify itself with a part of this appearance, a body. In doing so it 'forgets' itself and thereby appears to veil itself from itself.

The same is true as we wake in the morning, when the Peace of deep sleep still pervades our experience, before the appearance of separation has become fully established. The waking state emerges out of this Peace itself and is, for some time, saturated with it.

However, in most cases, Consciousness immediately and inadvertently loses itself in identification with a fragment. It condenses itself into a body/mind and the world is correspondingly projected 'outside.'

The illusion of separation reappears. One pretends to be two. Consciousness becomes a fragment, a 'me,' and the world correspondingly becomes 'other' and 'separate.'

Consciousness/Existence becomes Consciousness *and* Existence.

As a result of forgetting itself in this way, of apparently becoming an object, the Peace and Happiness that are experienced during this interval, that *are* this interval, are seemingly lost. The world then becomes their apparent abode, the place in which they can be sought and found.

Thus the search begins and the contracted 'me' becomes a seeker.

This contracted 'me,' which is simply Consciousness-pretending-to-be-a-separate-entity, overlooks or forgets that the experience of Peace and Happiness is inherent in its own nature. Instead it seems to become an intermittent experience that can be lost and therefore every time we have the experience of someone or something that once made us peaceful or happy, but now makes us agitated or unhappy, should be enough to indicate that Peace and Happiness are not delivered by objects.

Peace and Happiness are inherent in Consciousness.

Although Consciousness is always present and therefore Peace and Happiness are always present, under all circumstances, we do not always experience them.

However, it is not objects themselves that veil Peace and Happiness. It is the fact that we *think* and *feel* them to be objects, outside and separate from ourselves.

With this feeling that objects are on the *outside* and *separate*, comes the corresponding thought and feeling that 'I,' the presence of Consciousness, is on the *inside* and is similarly *separate*.

It is this division of the seamless totality of our experience into a perceiving subject and a perceived object that veils the Peace and Happiness that are present under all conditions and at all times.

It is for this reason that meditation is sometimes described as sleeping while we wake. In meditation we take the same attitude towards objects that we take in our sleep, that is, no attitude at all.

We simply abide as we are.

Most activities are governed by the desire for Happiness. Happiness is a non-objective experience. It is simply the presence of Consciousness.

As Consciousness is by nature conscious, it could be said that Happiness is the experience of Consciousness knowing itself knowingly.

It is the experience that is revealed every time a desire comes to an end. Desire is agitation and Happiness is the ever-present background of all states that is revealed when this agitation ceases.

Of course, it is also present during the agitation itself as it is the background of *all* states, but it is not experienced as such.

This desire for Happiness does not come from memory. Happiness cannot be remembered for it has no objective qualities. It is inherent in Consciousness, which in its unmanifest condition, is objectless, such as in the experience of deep sleep.

Consciousness cannot be experienced as an object and therefore cannot be remembered. However, it is always present and therefore whatever is inherent in it must also be ever-present.

The current object is continually changing but the *desire* for Happiness always remains the same. Therefore, Happiness cannot be caused by the *object* that is present.

Likewise the *experience* of Happiness is always the same, irrespective of the object that seems to deliver it, so the object itself cannot be the *aim* of the search for Happiness.

Once it is understood that Happiness cannot be a memory, it has to be concluded that the desire for Happiness comes *from* the current experience itself, even if the experience is unpleasant. Where else could it come from?

However, it is not from the *objective* aspect of the current experience that Happiness is sought. It is from the *knowing* or *experiencing* aspect.

The fact that Happiness is sought in such a wide variety of objects and activities indicates the intuition that Happiness resides in the *knowing* and *experiencing* aspects of an experience or an object, in the Consciousness aspect, not in the objective aspect, because the knowing or experiencing aspect of all experiences is always the same.

However, the knowing and experiencing aspect of experience is veiled by the name and the form of the experience, and therefore we keep looking for Happiness in new and different objects.

In fact our engagement with objects is, in most cases, precisely for the purpose of unveiling the Peace and Happiness that is inherent in every experience. However, we wrongly assign Peace and Happiness to the objective aspect of the experience.

Our exclusive focus on the objective aspect of experience veils this Happiness. However, failing to notice that Happiness is in fact already present, we search elsewhere for it. We search for it in a new situation, in a new object.

In fact even the desire for Happiness comes from Happiness itself.

Desire is the form of Happiness. It is the shape that Happiness itself takes when it overlooks its own presence and begins to search for itself elsewhere.

It is Happiness itself that seeks itself.

We are already what we seek.

What governs the type of object in which we search for Happiness will depend on the objects that, in the past, immediately preceded the non-objective experience of Happiness.

Unlike Happiness itself, these objects *can* be remembered and so we try to reproduce them in the hopes that they will deliver the same Happiness.

Once this is clearly seen, the nature of desire changes radically. An object is no longer desired in order to *produce* Happiness but rather to *express* it.

Once desire is liberated from the requirement to produce Happiness, it does not disappear. It is simply liberated from the confines of serving a non-existent entity.

Desire as such is experienced as energy, as life. It is already its own fulfilment.

Consciousness Is Self-Luminous

"When you see the sun rise, do you not see a round disc of fire somewhat like a guinea? Oh no, no! I see an innumerable company of the heavenly host crying, 'Glory, glory, glory is the Lord God Almighty.'"

WILLIAM BLAKE

The mirror of Consciousness is the screen on which everything is experienced and at the same time it is that which experiences everything.

The image that appears in the mirror is made only of mirror.

When a physical object is placed in front of a mirror, it colours the mirror and this colouring of the mirror seems to give the mirror object-like qualities. The mirror *seems* to take on the qualities of whatever is being reflected within it.

When the physical object vanishes the mirror again becomes colourless. In fact it was always only this.

Consciousness is transparent and cannot be seen as an object, in the same way that the glass out of which the mirror is made cannot be seen unless a physical object is reflected in it.

When a thought, a sensation or a perception is present, it 'colours' Consciousness in the same way that the reflection in the mirror colours the mirror.

The thought, sensation or perception reveals Consciousness in the same way that the reflection reveals the mirror.

The object that appears in Consciousness is nothing other than Consciousness, in the same way that the object that appears in the mirror is nothing other than mirror.

When we see an object – that is, when a thought, sensation or perception appears in Consciousness – Consciousness is experiencing itself. In fact, Consciousness is always only experiencing itself.

The metaphor of the mirror is helpful in that it enables us to understand that Consciousness cannot be experienced as an object.

However, unlike the mirror, Consciousness is conscious. It perceives. It experiences itself all the time, whether or not thoughts, sensations or perceptions are present.

The mirror needs a source *outside* itself to be seen, unlike Consciousness which is *simultaneously* that which sees *and* the screen on which it is seen. It is by definition always experiencing itself although, if no object is present, that experience has no objective qualities.

A more accurate metaphor would be that of a vast, limitless space of which every part is conscious, sensitive, aware.

The nature of this space is to be conscious. It cannot turn off this consciousness.

Imagine that within this limitless space, several holographic images, each of a house with many rooms, are projected. Each room is like a separate body/mind.

What happens to this limitless space when the hologram is projected? Does it change in any way?

What happens to the space when some of the images of houses are withdrawn and when new ones appear?

Is there anywhere in these images where space is not present?

Is the space that is contained within the apparent walls of the houses limited by those walls?

Is it not the same space inside, outside and within the walls themselves?

In fact there is no inside and no outside in this space because the houses are made out of exactly the same substance as the space in which they appear.

Even to say that the houses appear *in* the space is not quite right, because they do not come *into* the space. They *ex*-ist. They arise *out of* the space itself.

Their substance is *made* of that in which they arise. That which gives them *Existence* is the substance *out of* which they arise. The space *is* their *Existence*. They are *made* out of the substance of the space.

However, their *appearance* is the name and form of the house.

The same is true of our experience. The substance of all appearances is the Presence in which they arise.

The *Existence* of an object derives its Being from the Presence in which it arises. Its *appearance* is derived from its name and form.

That which sees *is* that which is seen.

The Consciousness which perceives the world is one with the Reality of the world.

Consciousness and Reality are one.

An experience consists of the *creation* of an 'object,' the *substance* of the 'object' and the *knowing* of the 'object.' These three are one, simultaneously.

The space of Consciousness is a knowing space. It is Self-luminous, Self-knowing, ever-present, Self-evident.

It knows itself in and as this current experience.

It is the Reality of all things and is its own Reality.

The Choice Of Freedom

Does the individual have free will?

Even conventional science tells us that there are no separate entities in the universe, that everything is interconnected, so the issue of whether or not an apparent separate entity has free will or choice is really not addressed here.

Rather we go straight to the question about the existence of the separate entity and, having explored it thoroughly, we see what happens to the question about free will and choice.

Nothing binds Consciousness, except its own desire to bind itself through belief.

Every experience arises spontaneously out of the absolute freedom of Consciousness at every moment, and in that sense Consciousness is free to take any form it chooses, out of an infinity of possibilities.

Every apparent choice is an expression of the absolute freedom of Consciousness. The sense of freedom and choice that we feel is an intuition of the innate freedom of Consciousness which, at some level, we know to be our own.

There is something oppressive about teachings that continuously reiterate the fact that we have no choice or freedom. Such a statement is directed at a non-existent personal entity and, ironically, in doing so, condones the very entity it denies.

It is true that the separate entity has no freedom, but as there is no separate entity, why mention it?

Consciousness, that which we are, is freedom itself. We, as Consciousness, have absolute freedom. We *are* absolute freedom.

The feeling that we have the freedom to make a choice is a pale and usually misinterpreted reflection of this intuitive knowledge of our own innate freedom.

As a *reflection* of real freedom it is true. Only the *interpretation* that this freedom is the freedom of an individual entity is false.

This exploration of the nature of experience takes place within Consciousness and is an expression of Consciousness.

There is no entity that does the exploring. Even from the point of view of scientific materialism there are no separate entities in the universe. Everything is interconnected.

If all the minds, bodies and worlds that exist are interconnected in one seamless system, how could the Consciousness, which is considered in scientific materialism to be a by-product of this system, itself be individual and separate?

And if there is no separate independent Consciousness, how can there be a separate, independent thinker, chooser, doer, enjoyer, experiencer?

Our experience is one of a stream of appearances in Consciousness. These events are thoughts, feelings, sensations and perceptions, one following another... A, B, C, D, E... Each is utterly unique and each disappears absolutely before the next arises.

Imagine a series of events as follows:

Event A is the hearing of rain. Event B is the thinking, "Let's have some tea." Event C is the tasting of tea. Event D is the feeling of satisfaction. Event E is the perceiving of traffic. Event F is the thought that 'I' didn't cause the rain but heard it, that 'I' chose to have tea and enjoyed it, that 'I' perceived the traffic but did not create it, and finally that 'I' remained over after all these experiences had vanished.

The 'I' in this stream of events is itself simply another appearance just like all the rest. The 'I' is the *thought* 'I.'

However, when the hearing of rain is present, the 'I' thought is not. Likewise when the thought, 'Let's have some tea,' is present, the 'I' thought is not. In between these two thoughts lies the timeless presence of Consciousness, the blue sky shining between the clouds. The 'I' thought is created to fill this interval, to impersonate the true 'I' of Consciousness.

This little 'I' thought then vanishes before the next thought, 'Let's have some tea,' appears, and reappears again after it, to fill the gap.

In this way innumerable 'I' thoughts are strung together and conceived, by a subsequent thought, to have existed as the permanent entity that is present between and behind all appearances.

However, it is Consciousness, not a separate entity, which is ever-present between and behind every perception.

The separate entity is created by and with the thought that thinks it, and is nothing other than that thought, in that moment. The next moment it vanishes, just like any other thought. It is an imposter!

To think that event F, the 'I' thought, did *not* cause event A, but *did* cause event B, is inconsistent with our experience and defies logic. This lack of consistency is called the 'person,' the 'separate entity,' the 'chooser.'

If we think in terms of cause and effect, we should say that A caused B, which caused C, which caused D, and so on. In other words, everything is linked together in a chain of causality.

Everything causes everything. The totality causes the totality at every moment.

Or we can say that everything arises spontaneously out of Consciousness and that Consciousness is therefore its sole and ultimate cause.

Both of these positions can be said to be true of our actual experience. In fact these two possibilities amount to the same thing, because the totality in the first position turns out, on further investigation, to be identical to Consciousness in the second position.

In fact the idea of causality falls apart completely when it is understood that experience is not a series of events appearing in Consciousness, but rather that it is Consciousness itself taking the shape of hearing, thinking, tasting, enjoying, perceiving, etc.

Our experience is not a series of events. It is one ever-present event, one ever-present non-event. Consciousness. Being. Reality. Immoveable, unchanging, homogeneous.

What is there to cause what, if Consciousness is all there is?

The Ease Of Being

Consciousness is not inherently identified with the body or the mind. Consciousness *is*, prior to the body, mind or world.

The natural condition of Consciousness is Freedom, Happiness and Peace.

When an object appears, it appears as a *modulation* of Consciousness.

Consciousness is simultaneously the substance and the witness of whatever appears.

However, Consciousness is not separate or removed from the object, perceiving it from a distance. When an object is present, that object is one with Consciousness. If they separate, the objective aspect vanishes utterly, instantly, whilst Consciousness remains as it always is.

Language cannot describe this, because even in attempting to describe it there is a reference to two things, the object and Consciousness. Two words are used whereas in fact there are never two things.

An object is the shape that Consciousness assumes, in the same way that a wave is the shape that water assumes.

Consciousness is one with every object. In fact, in the ultimate analysis, there are no objects. There is only Consciousness taking the shape of our experience from moment to moment.

The identity of an object is the identity of Consciousness.

An object could not appear if it was not one with Consciousness. Consciousness is every appearance, but that does not mean that Consciousness is limited to that appearance.

The 'I-am-the-body' idea arises in Consciousness, just like any other appearance and, as such, it is the form that Consciousness takes at that moment.

However, the fact that it arises in Consciousness doesn't necessarily make it true, any more than the thought that two plus two equals five, which also arises in Consciousness, is true.

It is an *expression* of Truth, but it is not true.

The sensation or cluster of sensations that are referred to as 'the body' seldom appears without some perception of the world also.

This conglomerate of sensations and perceptions is one seamless experience.

However, Consciousness arbitrarily divides this seamless experience of sensations/perceptions into two, into sensation *and* perception.

It does this by identifying itself exclusively with the sensations, with the body, and by disidentifying itself from the perceptions, from the world.

It thinks, "I am *this* cluster of sensations, the body, but not *that* group of perceptions, the world."

Therefore, it is not so much the 'I-am-the-body' idea but rather the 'I-am-*only*-the-body' idea that is problematic.

In order to remedy this exclusivity, some teachings suggest separating the perceiving Consciousness from the appearance of the body/mind, in order to establish that Consciousness stands alone and prior to all appearances.

This in turn paves the way for a more complete understanding, in which it is seen that experience is at every moment one seamless totality.

Consciousness is one with the *totality* of every experience, not just with a fragment, the body/mind.

In order to affect this second stage of understanding, Consciousness first disengages itself from its exclusive identification with a single body/mind, and comes to know itself as nothing, as not-a-thing, not an object or an appearance. It comes to know itself as the witness of all objects, before re-engaging with the *totality* of its experience and recognising itself as everything.

Consciousness transitions from, 'I am something' to 'I am nothing,' and then from, 'I am nothing' to 'I am everything,' without ever being or becoming anything other than itself.

However, this second stage is sometimes not emphasised in traditional teachings that tend to focus more on the witnessing aspect of Consciousness, the 'I-am-not-the-body' aspect, the 'I-am-nothing' aspect. This sometimes leads to a body-negative or experience-negative approach.

These teachings often make a goal of Nirvikalpa Samadhi, the experience of Consciousness knowing itself without an object, which has in most cases to be maintained through effort, in order to keep at bay what is considered to be the dangerous and distracting realm of thinking, feeling, sensing and perceiving.

However, it would be a misunderstanding to imply that by establishing Consciousness as the independent witness, distinct from the witnessed, a dualistic paradigm of subject and object is being condoned.

Without the recognition of the primacy and independence of Consciousness, there is nothing to suggest that there is anything more to experience than a continuous flow of appearances, and this understanding could be expressed as, 'There is only *this*,' meaning that there is only this current thought, sensation or perception.

However, once it is established, in experience, that Consciousness exists prior to and independent of all appearances, it can be seen clearly that it is only Consciousness itself that takes the shape of the flow of appearances, in which case in the statement, 'There is only *this*,' 'this' refers to Consciousness, not to objects.

This distinction is the difference between solipsism and wisdom, although both can be expressed by the same statement.

Returning to the identification of Consciousness with a fragment, there is a big difference between, 'I am not the body' and 'I am not *only* the body.'

'I am not the body' is true in that it suggests that 'I,' Consciousness, am not the body *if* by 'body' we mean an object that is outside and separate from Consciousness.

However, once it has been understood that all objects are like waves within Consciousness, that Consciousness takes the shape of every appearance, then 'I,' Consciousness, *am* the body. When the body is present it is Consciousness itself that is taking the shape of the body.

However, in this case it is still true that 'I,' Consciousness, am not *only* the body. 'I' am *also* the world and everything else that is appearing in that moment. 'I' am the *totality* of whatever is appearing within me, but 'I' am also more than that, just as the ocean is more than the sum total of the waves.

When no objects are present, Consciousness is naturally one with itself. When objects *are* present Consciousness is naturally one with whatever is present.

An object is limited when it is understood to be separate and independent of Consciousness, but it is infinite when understood to be an expression of Consciousness itself.

Consciousness *learns* to identify *exclusively* with one part of the totality of whatever appears within itself – that is, with a body/mind. It *chooses* this identification out of its own innate freedom. In that sense it is also natural.

Ignorance is a choice that Consciousness makes out of its own freedom.

However, this exclusive identification is not something that is chosen once and for all. It is something that we, Consciousness, choose from moment to moment. By the same token Consciousness is free to disidentify itself from the body/mind whenever it chooses.

Some spiritual traditions emphasise the efforts that are required by Consciousness to disidentify itself from the body/mind, but in fact Consciousness disidentifies itself effortlessly many times every day.

This disidentification takes place quite naturally and effortlessly every time we fall asleep and in the intervals between perceptions. Consciousness also disidentifies itself from the body/mind every time a desire is fulfilled.

Deep sleep is another example of the disidentification of Consciousness from the body/mind. In fact the Peace and Happiness that we experience in deep sleep is exactly the same Peace and Happiness that we feel on the fulfilment of a desire, or rather on the cessation of agitation that attends the fulfilment of a desire.

Consciousness, Happiness or Peace is like an underground river that bubbles up to the surface between the objects of the body, mind and world. It is a natural and familiar experience that is present in deep sleep and that is revealed on the cessation of a desire, during a moment of Love, Humour or Beauty and on many other occasions.

From the point of view of the mind these moments last for a period of time. They are considered to be caused by the objects that preceded them and to effect those that follow. They are seen to arise fleetingly to punctuate the seemingly continuous appearance of the body, mind and world.

However, from the point of view of Consciousness, it is *itself* the continuous Presence out of which the fleeting appearances of the body, mind and world bubble up from time to time, and is itself their cause.

These moments in between the appearance of objects are in fact timeless. They are neither linked together nor separated by time or space.

Happiness is not a fleeting appearance in the permanent substratum of time and space. Rather time and space are fleeting appearances within the permanent substratum of timeless, spaceless Presence.

Deep sleep is simply another name for this timeless, spaceless Presence. Like Happiness, it is causeless. Falling asleep is the most effortless thing. In fact it is impossible to make an effort to fall asleep. It is the *cessation* of a previous effort that allows deep sleep.

Exactly the same is true of Consciousness. The natural state is not to be exclusively identified with anything. It requires an effort to identify Consciousness *exclusively* with the body or the mind.

However, we have become so accustomed to this exclusive identification of our Self, Consciousness, with a body/mind that we are, in most cases, not even aware of the subtle effort that this identification requires.

For this reason Consciousness *seems* to have to make an effort to disidentify itself, but in doing so, it simply becomes aware of the previously undetected effort that it was making in order to *identify* itself exclusively with a body/mind.

This exclusive identification may be natural but it is not essential. Nothing imposes this exclusivity on Consciousness. Nothing compels it.

The state of identification with a single body/mind is part of Consciousness' repertoire, but it is not its original condition or its only possibility.

Consciousness is Freedom, and amongst the freedoms at its disposal is the freedom to identify or disidentify itself.

Its natural condition is free from exclusive identification, but it is free to identify itself exclusively with a body/mind, in order to enjoy and suffer what that has to offer.

Once Consciousness has identified itself exclusively with a body/mind, it seems to bind itself and, as a result, many of the subsequent experiences that appear within it seem to corroborate its new identity.

Finding itself apparently limited to a body/mind, it enjoys and suffers the inevitable consequences of being a fragment in a vast universe.

For some time it tries to manipulate its experience in order to yield Happiness, without yet understanding that Happiness and the separate entity are mutually exclusive positions.

However, after some time of playing the game of being a separate entity, Consciousness begins to tire. It longs for something more substantial than the fleeting and precarious moments of Happiness that seem to be at the mercy of innumerable causes that are apparently outside its control.

Having exhausted the conventional possibilities of securing Happiness, Consciousness-pretending-to-be-a-separate-entity searches in other, less familiar territory. One version of this is the spiritual search.

However, sooner or later, gradually or instantaneously, Consciousness comes to recognise that it is already precisely what it is looking for, and that it is the search itself that prevents this realisation.

This Self-recognition is not caused by anything that takes place within the search itself, because the Self-recognition is precisely the recognition that Consciousness *is* Happiness, Fulfilment or Peace itself, and that this Fulfilment is always and already prior to and within every experience.

This understanding is synonymous with the total collapse of the search, which may however reappear from time to time, due to the inertia of habit.

Consciousness is free to withdraw its exclusive identification with the body/mind whenever it pleases.

We forget that as an infant we gradually *learnt* to identify our Self, Consciousness, with successive levels of the body and the mind.

In most cases the withdrawal of this identification happens in reverse order, in a series of stages, starting with the most obvious layers of identification with the body and the mind, and continuing to the deepest layers.

We are like a deep well and the presence of Intelligence, Love and Beauty in our lives is like the appearance of the sun at midday, shining directly into the well.

Normally only the creatures living at the surface of the well are active, due to the lack of light, but for a short period each day, the creatures living at deeper levels wake up due to the presence of the sun shining directly above them.

Such is the presence of Intelligence in our lives. As the sun of Intelligence, Love and Beauty comes more frequently over the well, so deeper and deeper layers of identification come into the light and are revealed.

In this way Consciousness sees its identification with successive layers of the body/mind and clearly understands how it limits itself in this way. This understanding brings about a natural relaxation of this identification.

Every time it relaxes this identification, it is, without knowing it to begin with, remembering itself, returning to itself.

Consciousness never really returns to itself. It just abides knowingly in and as itself. It no longer pretends to be other than it is.

To begin with it is not accustomed to this abidance within itself and it grasps again for the old objects, the old habits of avoidance and resistance with which it has become familiar and comfortable.

However, over and over again this identification with layers of the body/mind is relaxed through understanding, and Consciousness becomes increasingly comfortable abiding in and as itself. The ease of Being begins to pervade experience.

From time to time old layers of identification with the body/mind reappear. However, they lose their separating power and with it their capacity to induce suffering.

Those that are necessary for the functioning of everyday life continue as and when they are needed. Those that are not functional drop away naturally and more and more we find ourselves in our natural condition.

This is not an extraordinary state. It is simple and natural, and may even dawn on us without the mind being aware of anything special.

In place of the subtle sense of lack that pervaded our thoughts, feelings and activities in the past, a sense of well-being and ease begins to shine in the background of our lives and to overflow into the foreground of our activities and relationships.

The experience of Love is precisely this relaxation of Consciousness' exclusive identification with a separate body/mind and, as a result, the inevitable inclusion of the other, of all 'others,' within itself.

For that reason Love is said and felt to be unconditional, uncaused, unmodified, universal. It has no opposite. It is inherent in our true nature.

Imagine a king who has enjoyed life in his palace. One day he wishes to experience the life of one of his subjects and so he instructs his ministers to treat him as a normal person until he commands them otherwise.

On the next day the king goes out into the market place disguised as a peasant and, although his ministers are watching from a distance, they are powerless to intervene.

To begin with the King does not notice that the enjoyment he feels in the market place is of the same nature as the enjoyment he feels in the palace, so he soon forgets that he is pretending.

Presently he begins to suffer and, having forgotten his birthright, tries all sorts of strategies within the market place in order to alleviate it.

However, nothing that is on offer can remind him or return him to his palace. Seeing his plight and feeling powerless to help, the ministers dress up as ordinary men. From time to time the King encounters one of his disguised ministers and, without betraying their promise to treat him as a normal person, they indicate to him that he is not what he thinks and feels himself to be.

Due to the depth of his amnesia, the King takes some time, but sooner or later, he remembers who he really is and returns to the palace, ordering the ministers to resume their official duties.

At the very moment the King abdicated his royal powers, he gave up his Freedom, of his own free will. His Freedom expressed itself as the desire not to be free. From that moment on he *seemed* to be bound and the circumstances of his life *seemed* to confirm his new status.

In this state, the only freedom available to the King-pretending-to-be-an-ordinary-person is the freedom to remember himself again, as he truly is.

It is only when the King reclaims his royal identity that he realises that although he thought, felt and behaved as though he were bound, in fact he was always free. He realises that his status as an ordinary person was self-imposed and imaginary, and that even when he was deeply involved with the traumas of being an ordinary person he was, nevertheless, always the King.

There was nothing that could be done or, more importantly, that needed to be done, to reclaim his birthright, other than simply to recognise it and to start behaving accordingly.

As the peasant, the King had no freedom other than to remember his true identity. As the King he always had complete freedom.

Once Consciousness has chosen, out of its own inherent Freedom, to identify itself with a fragment, the only freedom available to it is to disidentify itself from that fragment, to know itself again as it always is.

It is for this reason that the statements, 'You have no freedom,' and, 'You have complete freedom,' are both true, from different points of view.

Knowingness

The nature of Consciousness is knowing or Knowingness.

It is the *knowing* of what is known, the *experiencing* of what is experienced, the *perceiving* of what is perceived.

When Consciousness knows *anything* it knows *itself*.

Consciousness *is* the Knowingness in every experience, and therefore it knows itself in every experience, simply because it *is* itself.

Consciousness *is* the knowing of itself.

Consciousness does not have to *do* anything to know itself. Its being itself *is* its knowing itself. It *always* knows itself.

The sun's nature is to illumine. Therefore, by its nature it illumines itself. 'Illumination' is what it *is*, not what it *does*. It does not need to illumine itself, because by definition it is always illumined. It is self-luminous.

Likewise Consciousness is Self-luminous. It is the light with which it sees itself.

Knowing is what Consciousness *is*, not what it *does*.

Knowingness is the nature of Consciousness, therefore it knows itself in the knowing of anything.

In the knowing of any object, this knowing Consciousness is present and, as knowing is its nature, its presence *is* the knowing of itself.

Knowing and Being are identical in Consciousness.

It does not have to know *something* in order to know itself. Its knowing of anything *is* its knowing of itself.

And when no object is present, this knowing remains exactly as it always is, knowing only itself.

Consciousness cannot 'not know' itself.

When this is clearly seen Consciousness stops looking for itself outside itself, because it is deeply understood that it is experiencing itself in every experience that occurs.

When no objectivity is present – for instance in deep sleep or in the interval between thoughts or perceptions – Consciousness being itself *is* its knowing itself.

However, as no objective content is present in this experience, there is nothing to be remembered 'there.' Nothing objective is experienced, so the mind, which comprises only objects, cannot lay claim to this experience. It was not present during it. There was no mind and therefore nothing to be remembered.

As it reappears, the mind interprets this experience of the timeless presence of Consciousness as a blank, a void, because all it can know are objects. It would be more accurate to say that Consciousness represents this experience of its own formless presence, as a blank object in the mind. However, even a blank or a void is a subtle object.

As soon as this experience of the formless presence of Consciousness is represented in the mind, it takes a form, because mind *is* form.

Therefore, the most accurate representation in the mind of the formless presence of Consciousness, is a blank object, a void. It is, so to speak, a form without a form. It is a representation, which tries to impersonate the formless presence of Consciousness.

It is the best the mind can do but it is misleading because, by attempting to represent itself in the mind in this way, Consciousness commits itself to seeking for itself within the realm of objectivity.

In this way Consciousness is seduced by its own creativity. It creates this blank state as an impersonation of itself and then interprets that state as an absence of itself. In so doing, it believes its own creation of a blank object. It buys the, 'I am not present' theory, which Consciousness itself creates in the mind.

In short, Consciousness forgets itself.

As a consequence of buying the 'blank object' theory in this way, the 'I am not present' theory, Consciousness is condemned to looking for itself within the realm of objects.

This is the moment when the prodigal son leaves the palace. He turns away from the father towards the world of objects.

Consciousness apparently turns away from itself and looks outward towards the realm of mind.

In fact the experience of Consciousness knowing itself is always taking place. It is taking place in the absence of objectivity *and* in the presence of objectivity. That is why it is not quite true to say that Consciousness forgets itself. It would be more accurate to say that it *pretends* to forget itself.

The prodigal son leaves the palace, but he does not yet know that he never leaves the kingdom.

Therefore, because the experience of Consciousness knowing itself is colourless and transparent, because it cannot be experienced as an object, Consciousness overlooks its own Presence.

It forgets that it is always already experiencing itself and so it looks for itself outside, apparently outside, in the realm of objectivity.

In that moment, Consciousness throws a veil over itself, it forgets itself, and the search for itself begins.

Every now and then the search is brought to an end in a moment of Understanding, Love or Beauty. In such moments, Consciousness experiences itself knowingly.

Consciousness is reminded of itself. Consciousness reminds itself of itself. It tastes itself.

There Are Not Two Things

We only experience one thing.

There is only ever one experience present at any time. This alone is an invitation to see that Consciousness and Reality are one.

However, we misinterpret the nature of this experience. Suffering is another name for this misinterpretation.

From the conventional point of view our experience consists of a multitude of different objects, comprising various combinations of mind, body and world. That is, it comprises thoughts, images, bodily sensations and sense perceptions.

Each of these objects is usually considered to have independent existence. They are considered to be independent both from that which observes them and from one another.

We think that we experience 'ten thousand things' simultaneously, and that each of these 'things' comes, remains and goes in its own time, according to its character and the prevailing circumstances. For instance, we think that a mountain lasts longer than a tree and that a tree lasts longer than a thought.

However, none of these 'ten thousand things' is ever actually experienced as a discreet object. The totality of our experience at any moment is a seamless whole.

This seamless whole may seem to comprise a complex, compound object of mind, body and world, yet it is a cohesive, unified experience.

It may be complex but it is not fragmented. It is a *seamless* experience. It is *one* experience.

However, the mind fragments this seamless whole. It fragments the totality of our experience.

It abstracts single objects, such as a 'car' or a 'chair,' and confers the status of independent reality on each one. The object referred to as 'car' or 'chair' is a concept. It is not an experience. It is a useful concept but, nevertheless, it is a concept, not an experience.

The concept of the 'car' or 'chair' is itself part of the complex, multi-faceted object that is experienced, but we never actually experience the single object, the 'car' or the 'chair,' to which the concept refers.

In the process of this abstraction, the body and the mind are also conceptualised as objects that possess separate and independent existence which, although related to some of the other conceptual-ised objects, nevertheless have their own separate and independent reality.

This little enclave of objects called 'the mind and the body' is given special status in this process of abstraction. It is partitioned off from all the other conceptualised objects and, strangely, it is given the status of subject. It is considered to be 'me,' whilst all the other con-ceptualised objects, including of course everyone else, are considered to be 'other.'

We circumscribe certain objects with a boundary that is composed only of an idea. This idea seems to divide the seamless totality of experience into 'me' and 'not me.' Everything on the *inside* of this boundary is referred to as 'me,' and everything on the *outside* is referred to as 'the world,' as 'other.' However, this division never actually takes place.

A very simple experiment will show the falsity of this interpretation of experience. Place your hand on a nearby surface, such as a table. A new sensation will be generated by the contact of the hand and the table. It is a single sensation.

Now ask yourself, "Do I feel the table?" The answer is obviously "Yes." Now ask yourself, "Do I feel my hand?" The answer is obviously, "Yes." So in this experience we readily admit that we feel both our hand and the table.

However, is this new sensation that is generated by our hand touching the table two sensations? No, it is one. Yet we have acknowledged that both our hand and the table are experienced there.

Therefore, the new sensation that is experienced is neither 'hand' nor 'table.' It is not even correct to say that it is a *combination* of the 'hand' and the 'table' because, in such a statement, we are combining two conceptualised objects that are never experienced as such. They are non-existent as separate and independent entities.

To formulate the result of the experiment in these terms would be to use concepts that are themselves disproved by the very experiment that we are conducting.

So, let us call this new sensation that is generated by 'our hand touching the table,' sensation 'A.' Of course it is not possible to conduct this exact experiment in real life because it is not possible to isolate a 'hand' and a 'table.' There will always be other elements present.

Now, let us add one new element. Imagine that a blue wall is placed behind the hand on the table. A new sensation, which is now the combination of sensation 'A' with the 'blue wall,' will appear.

However, just as we concluded in the previous experiment, there is in this new experience no separate sensation 'A' nor a separate 'blue wall.' Both sensation 'A' and the 'blue wall' are concepts that are not actually experienced as such.

Similarly, to formulate our new experience as a combination of both 'A' and the 'blue wall' is again to use concepts that are disproved by the new experiment. So let us call this new sensation that is derived from the inclusion of the 'blue wall,' sensation 'B.'

If we carry on ad infinitum with this experiment, adding objects as we proceed, we will arrive at a sensation called sensation 'Z,' which comprises 'ten thousand things.' This would in effect be the totality of our current experience.

This experiment shows that we do not actually have the experience of separate isolated objects. The concept of separate isolated objects is an *interpretation* of our experience. It is not a *description* of it. The interpretation is a useful hypothesis but it is a mistake to confuse the interpretation for the actual experience.

This experiment demonstrates two facts about experience:

It shows that we do not experience 'ten thousand things.' We do not experience a *multiplicity* of objects. Two objects cannot exist at the same time. We experience 'one thing,' a multifaceted object comprising mind, body and world, and this 'one thing' refers to the totality of our experience at any moment.

The second thing that we learn from this exploration, is that the boundary line we draw around a small enclave within the totality of our experience, and which we label 'me,' is an arbitrary one. It bears no relation to actual experience. For instance, it is not possible to draw a clear line between the body and the world.

This is clearly seen if we ask ourselves whether sensation 'A,' the 'hand/table,' is on the *inside*, the 'me' side, or the *outside*, the 'other' side, of the boundary.

As 'hand' it is on the 'inside.' As 'table' it is on the 'outside.' And yet we have seen it is neither hand nor table. It is *one thing*. If it is one thing, one seamless experience, the line that divides it into 'me' and 'other' must be non-existent. This is our actual experience from moment to moment.

Another way to describe this last discovery would be to say that by removing the conceptual boundary between the 'me' and the 'not me,' we have reduced the status of what was previously considered the subject, 'me,' the mind and body, to the status of object, along with the rest of the world.

However, it is not even quite true to say that by removing the arbitrary boundary, the mind and the body are reduced to the status of object. For by removing this arbitrary boundary line, we simultaneously remove the categories of 'me' *and* 'not me,' the categories of 'subject' *and* 'object,' for one implies the other and cannot therefore stand alone.

We are left therefore with 'one thing,' the seamless totality of experience, before it is conceptualised into 'ten thousand things,' the raw Reality of our experience before the 'me' is arbitrarily divided from the 'not me,' before the notion of a subject and an object arise.

There are not two things.

However, it is also in fact going too far to say that there is 'one thing.' As soon as we make an object of it, a subject is implied, and again we are in the realm of duality, of two things. So, 'one thing' implies 'two things.'

As soon as we name it, however transparent the word we use, some degree of objectivity and, by implication therefore, subjectivity, is implied.

At the same time we have to recognise that whatever it is that we are trying to speak about, is not 'nothing.'

So let us refer to this as a 'seamless totality' or 'Oneness,' on the understanding that even these words confer a shadow of objectivity on that which cannot in any way be described by words or mind, and yet which itself illumines all words and minds.

Inherent in this 'seamless totality' of experience is the presence of a witnessing Consciousness. Whatever it is that experiences this 'seamless totality' is present by definition *within* that totality.

However, this witnessing Consciousness is not present within the experience as a little entity somewhere inside it, but rather throughout the *totality* of the experience.

There is no part of an experience where this witnessing Consciousness is not present.

In order to make a more thorough exploration of the nature of our experience, we will again draw an artificial line within the seamless totality of experience, within this 'Oneness,' and provisionally separate the witnessing Consciousness from the witnessed mind/body/world.

This separation is conceptual only, for the sake of clarity and understanding. It never actually takes place.

Within every experience there is *something* that perceives and there is *something* that is perceived, whatever that *something* is.

Whatever it is that *perceives* is referred to as 'subject' and whatever is *perceived* is referred to as 'object.'

We conceptually separate the Perceiver from the perceived in this way, although this time it is not the mind and the body that are the subject, the perceiver, and the world that is the object, the perceived. Rather, it is Consciousness that is the perceiving subject and the mind/body/world that is the perceived object.

Again, we are in the realm of duality, of subject/object relationship. However, this time we are closer to the facts of our experience. This time Consciousness is the subject and the mind/body/world is the object. Previously the mind and body was the subject and the world, including others, was the object.

In dividing experience in this way we are using the very same conceptualising powers of the mind that were initially responsible for dividing the unity of experience into a multiplicity of objects, of which a small enclave, the mind and body, were labelled 'me,' the subject, and the rest were labelled, 'not me,' the object.

So now we have divided the unity of experience into a subject, Consciousness, that witnesses, and an object, the mind/body/world, which is witnessed.

The objective aspect of experience is, in most cases, so engaging and compelling that the presence of Consciousness is usually over-looked.

In order to draw attention to this witnessing presence of Consciousness, we have artificially divided our experience into two. We divide 'Oneness' into a perceiving subject and a perceived object.

The objective aspect of experience, that which is known or perceived, changes at every moment. The subjective aspect of experience, that which knows or perceives, never changes.

Consciousness is that which experiences. We do not know *what* this Consciousness is but we know *that* it is. We know it is present, that there is something that is registering, witnessing, knowing the current situation.

Nor do we know exactly what the perceived object is, but we know that it exists, that is has Reality, Existence, Being.

In any experience we do not experience two things. Every experience is one.

Consciousness and its object are always one. There is no division between them.

Every objective experience is a seamless whole, Consciousness/object.

Therefore, having separated this seamless whole into subject and object for the purpose of establishing the presence and independence of this witnessing Consciousness, we take it a step further and re-establish the seamless whole. In fact we only reassert it, because it has always been such.

This could be called the return of the prodigal son. The moment of looking back towards the father is the moment of recognising that Consciousness is present.

Consciousness loses itself in the world of objects. The moment it turns its attention away from objects towards itself, it recognises itself. As it turns its attention more and more towards itself, it becomes absorbed in itself.

The moment the son takes a step towards the father, he begins to unite himself, his experience, with the father. The world of objectivity or, rather Consciousness-lost-in-the-world-of-objectivity, which is represented by the son, is reintegrated with the father.

In Reality, it is the father who comes running to meet the son. It is Consciousness that reclaims the world of objectivity.

Consciousness projects the world of objectivity from within itself and then reclaims that world.

The father knows that the son never leaves the kingdom, but the son – that is, Consciousness-believing-itself-to-be-an-object – has forgotten this, and so he has to return.

In reality the son is reclaimed, not returned.

There are not two things.

There is only Consciousness, Presence, Oneness.

Consciousness is the totality of our current experience, taking the shape of *this* current experience *now* and *now* and *now*.

Our experience is always only an expression of Consciousness. It is always only an expression of Oneness.

Its substance is always only ever Consciousness.

There is nothing other than this Consciousness taking the shape of our moment by moment experience and yet always remaining itself.

And when no experience is taking place, such as in deep sleep, the timeless interval between perceptions or on the fulfilment of a desire, Consciousness is still always only itself.

So we arrive at the same place we started. Our experience is the exactly the same as it always was and is, but our understanding, our interpretation, has changed. And because our interpretation has changed, it seems that our experience changes.

We started with the concept that the world contains the body, which in turn contains the mind, which in turn contains a little invisible

126

spark of Consciousness, which is at best considered to be a by-product of the world and at worst is overlooked altogether.

And we end with the understanding that Consciousness is the ever-present Reality of all things and that everything appears *within* it and as an expression *of* it.

We understand and feel that Consciousness witnesses and expresses itself simultaneously in every experience and that *that* is what we are, always changing, always the same.

Our experience is a seamless indivisible totality.

It is 'Oneness.'

It is simply 'experiencing.'

There are never two things that are experienced.

Our experience is always only Consciousness.

By reasoning in this way, the mind is brought to the limits of its knowledge. It is brought to see the falsity of its ideas and, in doing so, a new possibility becomes available, because Consciousness ceases to veil itself from itself with erroneous ideas.

It ceases to veil itself with its own creativity.

Consciousness looks in the mirror of experience and no longer sees the face of an 'other.'

It sees its own face.

It sees itself in all things and all things in itself.

Knowing Is Being Is Loving

Consciousness knows a thing by *being* that thing.

Consciousness cannot know anything that is not itself.

Consciousness sometimes identifies itself with the body and the mind. It bestows its own identity, the sense of 'I'-ness, which is inherent within itself, onto the objects of the body and the mind.

This identification comes from a true experience. Consciousness *is* one with everything that it experiences.

In fact Consciousness does not really *experience* a thing. It *is* that thing and its *being* that thing is its mode of *knowing* that thing.

It would be impossible for anything to exist in our experience that was not one with Consciousness.

Identity is inherent in Consciousness. Identification is 'being the same as,' 'being one with.'

Nothing is separate from Consciousness. Consciousness knows a thing by being one with it, by being that thing.

Therefore identification, in the sense of 'being one with,' is not a sign of ignorance. It is an inescapable fact of experience.

However, it is the *exclusive* identification of Consciousness with one part of the totality of its experience over and above another part, that is ignorant.

To remedy this exclusivity, Consciousness initially *disidentifies* itself from the body/mind.

Consciousness releases itself from this partial identification.

Consciousness withdraws the sense of 'me-ness from the body/mind, and allows it to return to its true abode, to itself.

We, Consciousness, take the position, 'I am nothing conceivable or perceivable.'

This is a pedagogical step that is taken in order to draw attention to the presence and primacy of Consciousness, and to indicate that Consciousness *is*, when objects are not present, as well as during their appearance.

However, we cannot really *return* identity to Consciousness because identity is always already inherent within Consciousness. That is what Consciousness *is*.

Nor can we withdraw identification from the body/mind. As soon as Consciousness is withdrawn from any object, that object, by definition, vanishes. It becomes non-existent.

There is never a true *object* of Consciousness and therefore Consciousness is never the *subject* of experience.

Consciousness and its object are always one, beyond the realm of subject and object.

In Reality there are no objects of Consciousness, but we grant the provisional status of objectivity to *all* appearances (including the body/mind) in order to relieve Consciousness' *partial* identification with the body/mind.

It is the 'I am the body/mind' belief that gives rise to the, 'I am not the world' belief. These two beliefs are co-created.

When Consciousness relieves itself of the belief and feeling that it is the body/mind, it simultaneously relieves itself of the belief and the feeling that it is *not* the world.

In this provisional state Consciousness is now free to identify itself with the *totality* of its experience, not just a fragment, not just a body/mind.

In fact Consciousness is *always* one with the totality of its experience, but this process is very powerful and it re-establishes the unity of all things in our actual experience.

Although Consciousness is always only the totality and never the fragment, although the unity is always established, we now *think* and *feel* that it is so.

Love is the name we give to Consciousness when it reawakens to its identity with all things, when it recognises itself *in* all things, *as* all things.

Love is the natural condition of Consciousness when it is knowingly one with all things.

It includes all things within itself and is itself the substance of all things.

Changeless Presence

There is something present which is experiencing the current situation. We do not know what that something is, yet we know for certain that it is present, that it is conscious.

We know that it is not the mind, the body or the world, because the mind, the body and the world are part of the current situation that is being experienced.

The mind, the body and the world appear *to* this witnessing presence of Consciousness.

If we try to find this Consciousness, if we turn our attention towards it, we are unable to see it or find it, because it does not have any objective qualities.

If it had objective qualities, these qualities would themselves be part of the current situation that is being experienced. They would be experienced *by* this witnessing presence of Consciousness. They would appear *to* it, along with all other objects.

At the same time, it is our direct experience that this witnessing presence of Consciousness is undeniably present. It is our most intimate Self.

It is what we know ourselves to be. It is what we call 'I.'

The current situation is changing all the time. Even if the changes are minute, nevertheless, from moment to moment we are presented with a different configuration of mind, body and/or world.

However, this conscious witnessing Presence, this 'I,' never changes. It is always simply present, open, available, aware.

Due to the inadvertent and exclusive association of Consciousness with the body and the mind, we tend to think that any change in the body and the mind implies a change in Consciousness.

However, if we look closely at our experience, we see clearly that we have never experienced any change in Consciousness itself.

If we look back over our lives we see that this conscious Presence has always been exactly as it is now. It has never changed, moved, appeared or disappeared.

The very first experience we ever had as a newborn baby was experienced by this witnessing presence of Consciousness. Consciousness was present to witness this first experience, but did we ever experience the *appearance* of Consciousness?

If the *appearance* of Consciousness was an experience there would have to have been another Consciousness present to witness this appearance. And if the appearance of Consciousness has never been experienced, what validity is there to the claim that Consciousness appears, that it has a beginning, that it was born?

Likewise have we ever experienced an end to Consciousness? If we experienced the disappearance of Consciousness, there would have to be another Consciousness present to witness this disappearance. And this 'new' Consciousness, which witnessed the disappearance of the 'old' Consciousness, would have to be present during *and* after its disappearance, in order to make the claim legitimately that it witnessed its disappearance.

Therefore we cannot claim that we ever have the experience of the disappearance of Consciousness, and so what validity is there to our conviction that we, as Consciousness, die?

We experience a beginning and an end to all objects, but we never experience a beginning or an end to Consciousness, to our Self.

We may think that Consciousness disappears when we fall asleep and reappears on waking, but this is in fact not our experience. It is an uninvestigated belief.

However, it is a belief that has taken hold so deeply and become so much a part of the accepted norm, that we actually *think* that we experience the disappearance of Consciousness when we fall asleep.

As we fall asleep we first experience the withdrawal of sense perceptions or, more accurately, the faculties of perceiving and sensing. With the disappearance of perceiving, the world vanishes from our experience, and with the disappearance of sensing, the body vanishes from our experience, leaving only thinking and imagining. This is the dream state.

The thinking and imagining functions are in turn withdrawn and, as a result, the dream state gives way to deep sleep.

In deep sleep Consciousness simply remains as it always is, open and aware, only there are no objects present within it.

Consciousness projects the appearance of the mind, body and world by taking the shape of thinking, sensing and perceiving.

The process of falling asleep is not one of a separate entity transitioning through states. It is simply the withdrawal of this projection.

Due to the fact that we have so closely and exclusively identified Consciousness with the body and the mind, we presume that the absence of the mind and body during the experience of deep sleep implies an absence of Consciousness.

However, that is simply the mind's interpretation of an experience during which it was not present. It is a presumption based on a presumption.

It is a presumption that Consciousness is in Reality exclusively identified with the body and the mind, and this in turn gives rise to another presumption that Consciousness disappears when the body and mind disappear on falling asleep and, by implication, when the body dies.

This is not our experience in the first case and there is no evidence to suggest that it will be our experience in the second.

There is evidence that sentience disappears on death, but not that Consciousness disappears.

After a period of deep sleep, the Consciousness that was present there takes the shape of thinking and imagining and, as a result, the dream state reappears.

And in turn, after a period of dreaming, Consciousness takes the shape of sensing and perceiving and, as a result, the body and the world are recreated – that is, the waking state reappears.

If we look at deep sleep from the point of view of the waking state, it appears to have lasted a certain length of time, in the same way that the objects that appear in the dream and waking states appear to last for a certain length of time.

Time is the imagined duration between one appearance and another. There are no appearances during deep sleep and therefore time is not present there.

In fact time is not even present in the dreaming and waking states but at least the *illusion* of time is present in these states. In deep sleep not even the illusion of time is present.

Time, in the waking and dreaming states, is an illusion. In deep sleep, it is a presumption.

The language of the waking state is based on objects and time and, therefore, when we view dreamless sleep from the point of view of the waking state, we think that it must have lasted for a certain duration, because the mind cannot imagine timelessness.

The mind construes that the time it *imagines* to be real is an *actual* experience. It imagines that time is present in the absence of mind, in the absence of itself, and therefore imagines that deep sleep has duration. Deep sleep is therefore considered to be a state.

However, divested of duration, deep sleep is in fact the timeless presence of Consciousness that is beyond, behind and within all states and, although it gives birth to the *appearance* of time, it is not itself *in* time.

Our experience is that deep sleep is simply the timeless presence of Consciousness that does not appear or disappear.

Does that which is present during deep sleep or, rather, that which is present *as* deep sleep, disappear when the dreaming world appears?

No! The dreaming world simply emerges *within* deep sleep – that is, within this timeless Consciousness.

Does that which is present *as* deep sleep disappear when the world of the waking state appears?

No! The waking world simply emerges *within* deep sleep, *within* this timeless Consciousness.

The transition from deep sleep to dreaming to waking is seamless. In fact it is not a transition at all. It is presumed to be a transition only from the point of view of the waking state where a separate entity seems to transition from one state to another.

However, from the point of view of Consciousness there is no transition, there is simply a flow of changing appearances, and sometimes no appearances at all, in its own ever-present Reality.

That which *is* deep sleep, timeless Presence, does not disappear in order for the dreaming and waking worlds to appear. It simply remains as it always is and, at the same time, takes the shape of the dreaming and waking worlds.

At no point in this process does a separate entity fall asleep or transition from one state to another.

Nobody falls asleep and nobody wakes up.

When viewed from the perspective of the waking state, deep sleep is a state. When viewed from its own perspective, it is timeless Presence.

Time Never Happens

All we have is experience.

The mind is simply the *experience* of the mind. The body is simply the *experience* of the body. The world is simply the *experience* of the world.

We conceptualise a mind, a body and a world that exist outside, separate and independent of experience, that are considered to exist when they are not being experienced. However, such a mind, body and world have never been experienced.

Nor would it be possible to have such an experience because, as soon as it is experienced, it would, by definition, fall *within* experience and would therefore no longer be outside, separate from or independent of it.

Experiencing is the essential ingredient of the mind, the body and the world, and Consciousness is the essential ingredient of experiencing.

What would the mind, the body and the world look like if experiencing were removed from them?

And what would experiencing look like if Consciousness was removed from it?

Every experience that has ever occurred always occurs 'Now.' The past and the future are in fact never actually experienced. Thoughts and images *about* the past and future are experienced, but they always appear 'Now.'

In fact time is never experienced. Only 'Now' is experienced. Time is a concept, albeit a useful one, but it is not an experience. The *concept* of time is an experience but time itself is not.

'Now' is ever-present. Was there ever a time that was not 'Now'? 'Now' is not a moment. A 'present moment' is never experienced.

A 'present moment' implies an infinitesimally short duration of time. Duration implies a before and an after, a past and a future. The 'present moment' is normally considered to be one of innumerable such moments that arise in succession ad infinitum.

The concept of time has been created to 'house' these apparent moments, which are considered to arise *in* time. And time itself is considered to have existed 'for ever,' outside and independent of the Consciousness that apparently experiences it.

However, if we look at our experience and refuse to admit concepts that do not correspond directly with it, we see clearly that this model of time simply does not reflect its nature.

All experience is 'Now' and 'Now' is ever-present.

However, language is so conditioned by abstract and erroneous views of time and experience, that it is impossible to use it to convey the Reality of our experience. For instance, the term 'ever-present' is used to describe the 'Now,' but 'ever' already implies duration in time, and 'present' implies a past and a future.

'Eternity' is a word that is used to indicate this 'ever-present Now,' and although it has become associated with an infinite period of time, in its original meaning it is perhaps the closest word that is available to convey the immediacy and Reality of 'Now.'

Divested of its false association with an imagined 'time,' the 'Now' is experienced simply as it is, timeless Presence.

When an experience is present, it is the 'Now' that has taken the shape of that experience. It *is* that experience.

When the object vanishes the 'Now' simply remains what it always is, Presence, Consciousness.

The 'Now' is the substance and container of all experience.

Time, divested of the illusion of duration, is Consciousness.

Consciousness creates the appearance of time by bestowing its own continuity on objects and then forgetting that it has done so.

However, just as Consciousness chooses to forget itself, it also chooses to remember itself. Consciousness stops pretending to be other than itself. It withdraws its projection from objects.

It gives itself back to itself.

Every time Consciousness ceases to take the shape of the mind, the body and the world, it knows itself again as Presence or Being.

In fact it is always only knowing itself, even in the presence of objects, only now the clear glass of Presence is no longer coloured by apparent objectivity.

These 'moments' of Self-recognition are devoid of objective content and are therefore timeless. They leave no trace in memory.

These 'moments' in between the appearance of objects, whether thoughts, images, sensations or perceptions, are conceived of as gaps of minute duration that appear within the flow of experience.

However, this formulation is a concession to the mind that can only think in terms of objects. It is a hint that Consciousness gives itself to remind itself of its true nature.

Once Consciousness has, by taking thought, convinced itself that it appears in time and space, and that time and space are not appearances within itself, it then takes this conviction for granted, for real. Consciousness binds itself with this conviction.

All subsequent formulations presume this fundamental reality of time and space, and when Consciousness now creates an image of itself through thinking, it does so in terms of this new belief. Hence the idea that Consciousness appears as momentary gaps in between the flow of objects in a never-ending substratum of time and space.

In fact it is the objects that appear momentarily in a never-ending substratum of Consciousness.

And it is the presence of objects that implies the illusion of time and space. When objects are not present, it is not an infinite extension of time and space that remains. It is Presence, *prior* to time and space, that remains.

In the teachings of Non-Duality, it is sometimes suggested that attention is given to these 'gaps' between perceptions. These gaps are undoubtedly present, for without them one thought or perception would never come to an end and another would never begin.

However, they are not gaps that have duration in time, because there is no time between perceptions.

If Consciousness, in the form of mind, is convinced that it is not present, that something is missing, that something needs to be done or found in order to return to itself, then turning the attention towards these 'gaps' between perceptions is very powerful.

Consciousness thinks that it is not present and that it needs to find itself. It has forgotten that the idea that time and space exist independently of objects, that they are the substratum of experience, is a concept not an experience.

To begin with this 'gap' is conceived of as a blank object, a 'nothingness.' However, conceiving itself in this way, Consciousness is simply creating as close an approximation to itself as is possible within the mind, because Consciousness cannot conceive of itself as something that is not an object.

This gives it something to look for, something that has no qualities and yet that seems to appear in time and space which are still, at this stage, considered absolute realities.

Consciousness conceives of itself as a subtle object towards which it can turn. It does not yet know that it is *already* the attention that it is trying to give itself.

It does not yet see clearly that attention divested of an object is already Consciousness, Presence, itself. So it plays a trick on itself. It searches for itself.

Consciousness never finds itself in this way because it is, without knowing it, already itself.

However, in attempting the impossible task of using mind to look towards that which is not an object, Consciousness is somehow undermining its habit of looking 'outside' and 'elsewhere.'

The mind dissolves when it tries to see or touch that objectless place. The search collapses. It is undermined rather than fulfilled.

In fact it is not so much that the mind dissolves but rather that Consciousness, which had assumed the form of a separate limited entity through identifying itself with a body and a mind, relieves itself of this identification. As a result, it recognises itself, realises itself, remembers itself, experiences itself, not in the disguise of mind, but directly and knowingly.

Consciousness realises that it does not *receive* attention, it *gives* attention. And subsequently it realises that it does not *give* attention. It *is* attention.

Attention is Consciousness with an object. When the object vanishes, attention simply remains what it always is, Consciousness.

Consciousness is already the shape of every object towards which it turns. It witnesses and manifests itself simultaneously *as* that object.

It recognises itself.

Unveiling Reality

Whatever the characteristics of the current experience, the *Reality* of it, its essential nature, is present and unchanging.

Reality is not available in some future occasion nor it is dependent on specific circumstances. Whatever Reality is, it is present at every moment.

This experience is real and *this* experience is real and *this* experience is real.

Each of these experiences was different, objectively, albeit only slightly. Yet the *Reality* of each experience, the *Existence* of each of those three experiences, is identical and ever-present.

The changing character of experience *veils* its Reality and, at the same time, the *presence* of experience *is* its Reality.

That part of an experience that appears, both *veils* and *expresses* that part of an experience which does *not* appear, and yet which is present.

Every experience seems to both veil and reveal Reality.

Experience, as appearance, is always changing, disappearing. Experience, divested of appearance, stands revealed as Being.

At every moment, appearances are changing, one appearance is disappearing after another. At every moment appearance is vanishing, revealing the continuum of Being.

Being *is*, both behind and within appearances.

The Being that shines in all experience is known in ourselves as the experience, 'I am.'

In the world it is known as, 'It is.'

We share the Presence that we are with all things.

We Are What We Seek

Consciousness is the primal and most intimate fact of experience.

Every experience that we ever have, that we ever could or will have, is experienced *by* this Consciousness.

Meditation is simply to abide knowingly as this presence of Consciousness.

It is very easy because we already *are* that. In fact it would be impossible to be anything else.

In meditation we just remain as we are, as we always have been, and we allow the mind, the body and world to be just as they are.

The presence of the mind, the body and the world, however peaceful or agitated, is only possible because of this witnessing presence of Consciousness.

Nothing can obscure Consciousness. Nothing can obscure this witnessing Presence.

It does not matter if thoughts arise, if attention is apparently diverted by thoughts, by sensations in the body or by an occurrence in the world. It is only possible to have these experiences because Consciousness is present.

The mind, the body and the world do not obscure Consciousness. They indicate it. They reveal it. They express it.

In meditation the mind is allowed to be exactly as it is, without the need to change it. There is no need to make it peaceful, no need to stop the thoughts, no need to make them positive.

We just remain as we are, allowing our experience to be whatever it is from moment to moment.

If we find ourselves exclusively engaged with one aspect of our experience, for instance, if we are preoccupied with a thought or something in the world, it usually suggests that we are trying to get rid of or hold on to that object. We either like it and want to keep it, or we dislike it and want to get rid of it.

However, once we have understood that the acquisition or loss of an object does not in any way implicate Consciousness, we just go back to our Self, to this conscious Presence. As we are that already, this simply means that we return there knowingly.

We *seem* to return there, but in fact we just *remain* there knowingly. We abide there.

Experience is allowed to flow. It is allowed to move and change. If we find ourselves trying to manipulate it, that is fine. That is also part of the current experience. It is allowed to be.

In time the first layer of resistance, the 'I don't like,' dies down, but that is not the purpose of meditation.

There is no purpose to meditation. The purpose is already accomplished.

We are already what we are. We are already what we seek.

We just abide as that.

To begin with, as we take a step back from the objects of experience, we experience ourselves as Consciousness, Presence.

Later on we discover that Peace and Happiness are inherent qualities of this Presence. They come from the background of Consciousness not from the foreground of objects.

However, it is artificial to divide our experience into two, into Consciousness and the mind/body/world, into the subject 'I' and the object, the mind/body/world.

The reason for doing this is not to *describe* the Reality of our experience but rather to draw attention to the presence and primacy of Consciousness.

Normally we are lost in objects, in the mind, body and world, and we are not even aware of the presence of Consciousness. So in order to see clearly that Consciousness is present in every experience, we take a step back, so to speak, from the objects of the mind, body and world.

By doing this we establish that not only is Consciousness *present* in every experience, but that it is our *primary* experience.

Once we have established the presence of Consciousness as a fact of actual experience, we can take another look at the mind, body and world from the point of view of Consciousness.

Where do our thoughts appear? Do they just appear *to* Consciousness or do they appear *in* Consciousness?

If they appear *to* Consciousness rather than *in* Consciousness, there would have to be a clearly perceived border or interface between the perceived thought and the perceiving Consciousness.

Do we experience such a border? Look at a thought now. Is it separate from Consciousness? Is there a place where they meet?

No! There is no dividing line between the two. The thought obviously occurs *within* Consciousness.

We can do the same experiment with a bodily sensation. Take the tingling sensation of the face.

Where does that sensation appear? Is there an interface between the sensation and Consciousness? Does it not appear in the same place as thoughts appear? Does it not appear not just *to* Consciousness but *within* Consciousness?

We should not believe the story that the mind tells us about what and where the body is. We should rely only on the facts of our experience and that means this current experience. That is the test of Reality, of Truth.

In this investigation we have to be innocent like a child and honest like a scientist. Innocent in the sense that we take every experience as if we were experiencing it for the first time, which is in fact the case. And honest in the sense that we stick to our actual experience and discern what we *think* we experience from what we *actually* experience.

We can conduct the same experiment with the world, with our sense perceptions.

For instance, take a sound that would normally be conceptualised as taking place at a distance. Refuse any story that the mind tells us about the nature and whereabouts of that sound.

Does it not occur in the same place as the thoughts and sensations? Does it not arise within Consciousness? Are the sound and Consciousness not one seamless experience? Is the sound at a distance from Consciousness, separated from it? Is there a border or interface between the sound and Consciousness? No!

When thoughts, sensations and perceptions appear, they appear *in* Consciousness not just *to* Consciousness.

Our experience is one seamless totality. The Consciousness and the thought, sensation or perception, are *one* experience.

We are deeply conditioned to believe that the world contains the body, that the body contains the mind and that the mind contains a little intermittent spark of Consciousness. And because this conditioning is so deep, we *feel* that this is so.

However, we never experience a body in a world, a mind in a body or Consciousness in a mind.

It is not the world that contains the body, the mind and Consciousness. It is Consciousness that contains the mind, the body and the world, on an equal footing.

The mind, the body and the world appear *in* Consciousness. That is our actual experience. It is not an extraordinary experience. It is not the experience of one in a million enlightened sages. It is just our natural, every day experience. It always has been. When it is seen, it is so simple and so obvious.

The old belief that the world contains the body, which contains the mind, which contains Consciousness, triggers a series of thoughts, feelings and activities all based on that belief.

Once it is seen clearly that it is Consciousness that contains the mind, the body and the world, these thoughts, feelings and activities slowly unwind. They disappear, not through any effort but rather through neglect. They simply become redundant. Their foundation has been removed.

The clear seeing that everything is within Consciousness is instantaneous. The unwinding of old habits of thinking, feeling and acting, takes time.

This exploration about the true nature of experience can be taken further. Once it is seen clearly that thoughts, bodily sensations and

149

world perceptions appear *in* Consciousness, we can investigate what is the actual *substance* of that experience, of that object.

Take a thought, for instance. Is its substance different from the Consciousness in which it appears?

Is there any difference between the actual sensation of the tingling in our fingers and the Consciousness in which it appears?

Take a sensation, a sound, a texture, a taste or a smell. See that each appears *within* Consciousness and then go deeply into the actual experience itself and see what it is made of.

Is it made of a substance that is different or distinct from the Consciousness in which it appears? Is there any difference between the actual sensation or perception and Consciousness itself?

Can you find another substance, in actual experience, out of which the sensation or perception is made? If there is another substance, it must itself be a thought, image, sensation or perception. Just repeat the same experiment with it, until it becomes absolutely clear and obvious that there is no substance to experience other than this very Consciousness.

It is easiest to begin with thoughts, because even in ignorance thoughts are considered to appear within us and they are obviously not physical. However, the whole field of sensory perceptions can be explored in this way and each of them in turn is revealed to be made only of Consciousness.

The visual realm is perhaps the one that seems to appear outside most convincingly. However, the visual realm is a perception. It is made out of perceiving, out of mind, which as we have seen with thoughts, is nothing other than Consciousness. There is no difference.

The very substance of every experience is the substance of Consciousness.

Objects do not just appear *in* Consciousness they appear *as* Consciousness

Consciousness does not just *witness* every experience, it *expresses* itself as every experience.

Everything that is experienced is experienced *by, through, in* and *as* Consciousness.

Consciousness witnesses, experiences and expresses itself from moment to moment, and when there are no objects present, it simply remains as it always is.

That is all there is.

Presence.

This.

Nature's Eternity

Does art have any value or relevance in the investigation into or expression of the nature of Reality?

Paul Cézanne said, "Everything vanishes, falls apart, doesn't it? Nature is always the same but nothing in her that appears to us lasts. Our art must render the thrill of her permanence, along with her elements, the appearance of all her changes. It must give us a taste of her Eternity."

That statement must be one of the clearest and most profound expressions of the nature and purpose of art in our era.

What did Cézanne mean, standing in front of a mountain, Mont St. Victoire, one of the most solid and enduring structures in nature, when he said, "Everything vanishes, falls apart..."?

Cézanne was referring to the act of seeing.

We do not perceive a world outside Consciousness. The world is our *perception* of the world. There is no evidence that there is a world outside the perception of it, outside Consciousness.

The seen cannot be separated from seeing and seeing cannot be separated from Consciousness.

A solid object cannot appear in Consciousness any more than a solid object can appear in thought.

Only an object that is made out of matter could appear in space. Only an object that is made out of mind could appear in mind. And only an object that is made out of Consciousness can appear in Consciousness.

And as everything ultimately appears in Consciousness, everything is, in the ultimate analysis, made out of Consciousness.

When we say that we perceive an object, we mean that that object appears in Consciousness. It is a perception appearing in Consciousness.

If we close our eyes for a moment, the previous perception vanishes completely. If we reopen our eyes a new perception appears. Although it may seem to be the same object that reappears, it is in fact a new perception.

If we repeat this process, apparently looking at the same object over a period of time, the mind will collate the various images or perceptions and conceive a solid object that has apparently endured throughout the appearance and disappearance of the perceptions, and that exists in time and space, independently of the Consciousness that perceives it.

This concept will itself appear and disappear like any other perception. And with the next thought, a subject, a viewer, will be conceived, which allegedly had several different views of the apparent object, and which was allegedly present before, during and after its appearance.

In this case the object and the viewer, which are both conceived as existing in their own right, independent of the thought that thinks them, are both concepts.

Such an object and its subject, the viewer, are in fact simply and only that very thought with which they are conceived.

And in order to conceive of such an object that exists and endures in time and space, time and space themselves have first to be conceived, in order to house these objects.

Likewise, time and space themselves turn out to be nothing other than the very thought with which they are conceived.

However, although this capacity of mind to conceive an object and a corresponding subject is useful, it does not reflect an accurate model of experience.

Our actual experience is that one perception disappears *absolutely* before the next perception appears. It is in this sense that, as Cézanne said, everything 'vanishes' from moment to moment.

The apparent experience of a solid object is dissolved in this understanding, and is replaced by the understanding that we in fact experience a series of fleeting, insubstantial perceptions. It is in this sense that 'everything falls apart.'

Having said that, we also have the deep intuition that *something*, which Cézanne calls 'nature,' endures.

Where does this sense of endurance or permanence come from? From where does Cézanne derive the knowledge that, 'Nature is always the same,' given that he has already acknowledged that, 'Everything we see vanishes, falls apart'?

As human beings we are just as much a part of nature as the mountain that Cézanne was looking at. The body/mind/world is one integrated system.

Therefore, the exploration of the so-called internal, subjective realm of ourselves and of the so-called external, objective realm of nature must, in the end, lead to the same Reality.

Nature and man are part of one integrated system and must therefore share their Existence. Their Being must be shared.

Looking at the objective aspect first, Cézanne acknowledges that the sense of endurance or permanence in nature cannot come from 'the appearance of all her changes,' because 'nothing in her that appears to us lasts.'

He implicitly acknowledges that an 'object' is a concept derived from a series of fleeting, insubstantial perceptions, but that each of those perceptions has a shared Reality. This Reality is *expressed by* but is *independent of* each of those appearances.

In his statement that 'Nature is always the same but nothing in her that appears to us lasts,' there are three elements.

There is the *Reality* or *Existence* of nature, which is 'always the same.' There is the *appearance* of nature, in which 'nothing lasts.' And there is the 'us,' that is, *Consciousness*, which is aware of the appearances.

Cézanne acknowledges these three elements in any experience. Existence, appearance, Consciousness.

From which of these three elements does Cézanne derive the knowledge that in our experience of nature there is *something* that is 'always the same,' that there is *something* that endures?

In the statement, 'Nothing in her (nature) that appears to us, lasts,' Cézanne discounts whatever *appears* in nature as a possible source of that which is 'always the same.' This leaves only Existence and Consciousness.

What is the relation between these two, Existence and Consciousness, and in what way can one or both of them account for what Cézanne describes as, 'that which is always the same'?

Nature appears to us as form and concepts. Form is the raw data of the sense perceptions and concepts are the labels or interpretations, pieced together by the conceptualising power of mind.

There is also an element in our experience of an object or of nature, that *is*. Nature has *Existence, Reality* or *Being*. It *is*.

Although the appearances are changing all the time, their Existence or Reality doesn't change from one appearance to another.

This Existence is not an intellectual theory. Although it cannot be *perceived* as an object, nevertheless it is *expressed* and *experienced* in every experience that occurs.

Cézanne calls this Existence or Beingness, which is always present and yet does not appear, 'Eternity.'

Having discounted 'that which appears' as the source of nature's Eternity, its only other possible source is either *Existence, Being,* the *Isness* of things, or Consciousness.

Existence or Being is present in every experience of an object and does not change or disappear when forms and concepts change and disappear, any more than water ceases to be water when a wave disappears.

There is a *Reality* to every perception although the perception itself is fleeting and insubstantial, vanishing at every moment, and this Reality endures from one appearance to another.

This Reality is the support or ground of the appearance. The appearance may be an illusion, but the illusion itself is real. There *is* an illusion. It has Reality.

The Reality of any experience is not *hidden* in the appearance, it is *expressed* by the appearance.

If we deeply explore the nature of any experience, we find that this Reality is its *substance*. It is the *content* of the appearance.

In fact it is only Reality that is ever, actually experienced.

Before this is evident, we see only appearances. After it is evident we see the appearance and the Reality simultaneously.

We do not see anything *new*. We *see* in a new way.

For instance, we may mistake a rope for a snake. The appearance, the form and concept of the apparent snake does not describe the Reality of the rope.

However, the Reality of the rope is the *substance of* and is *expressed by* the snake. There is something that is real in our experience of the snake. It is the rope.

The rope is not *hidden* by the snake. In fact we only ever see the rope.

That which *appears* as snake *is* rope.

The experience of the appearance of the snake *is* the experience of the rope, only it is not known as such.

Fear of the snake is the natural outcome of this lack of clarity, and it vanishes instantaneously when the Reality of the rope is seen.

The snake cannot appear without the rope. The rope is the real substance, the Reality, of the appearance of the snake. Without the rope there would be no snake but without the snake, which never existed in the first place, there is still a rope.

So we know that nature is real, that there is *something* present, that there is a Reality to it, even if everything that *appears* to us is insubstantial and fleeting.

Whatever is real, by definition, endures. Something that is not present cannot be said to be real. Only that which is truly present can be said to be real, to have Reality.

We experience this vividly every time we wake from a dream. The appearance of the dream *seemed* to be real but on waking we discover that it was only a fleeting appearance within Consciousness.

The tiger in our dream seems to be real but on waking we discover that it was made of mind, and mind simply comprises appearances in Consciousness.

Consciousness is the Reality of mind. The tiger in the dream is unreal as 'tiger' but real as Consciousness.

When the tiger is present there is a Reality to it. The Reality of the tiger is Consciousness, which is its support, its substance and its witness.

Consciousness is not obscured by the tiger. It is Self-evident in the tiger. It knows itself *in* and *as* the appearance of the tiger.

Our objective experience in the *waking* state also comprises fleeting appearances in Consciousness. Therefore, in the ultimate analysis, there is no difference between the two states of dreaming and waking.

The substratum and the substance of the appearances in the dream *and* the waking states, their *Reality*, is identical and it remains after appearances have vanished.

The appearance is made only of its underlying Reality. The image in the mirror is made only of mirror.

This Reality is always present. We have never experienced its absence. And we have never experienced anything other than this Reality.

Change is in appearance only. There is only Reality taking the shape of this, and this and this.

How could something that is real become unreal? Where would its Reality go?

How could something whose *nature*, whose *substance* is Reality, become something else, become non-reality?

Whatever is real in our experience of nature or indeed of any object, whatever endures, whatever is truly experienced, is undeniably present in *every* experience.

Reality is the substance of every experience. It is the Existence, the 'Beingness,' the 'Isness,' the 'Suchness,' the 'Knowingness,' the 'Experiencingness,' in every experience.

And even when there is no objectivity present, such as in deep sleep or in the interval between appearances, this Reality remains as it always is.

This formless Reality is concealed or revealed by appearances depending on how we see.

Being without form, it cannot be said to have any limitations, because any limitation would have to have a form, would have to be experienced through the mind or the senses, in order to be an objective experience.

At the same time, what is being described here is an intimate fact of experience. There is something real in this experience now.

What is it in our experience that is undeniably and continuously present and yet has no external qualities?

The only answer to that question from our direct experience is Consciousness. Consciousness is undeniably experienced during any appearance and yet it has no objective qualities.

Therefore, Consciousness *and* Reality or Existence are both present in every experience.

What is the relationship between Consciousness and Existence?

If they were different there would have to be a border, a boundary between them. Do we experience such a boundary?

No! We have already acknowledged Consciousness and Existence, from our own intimate experience of both, as being undeniably present and also as having no objective defining qualities.

If they have no objective qualities how can they be said to be separate or different? They cannot!

Therefore, whether we realise it or not, in our actual experience they are one, Consciousness/Existence, not Consciousness *and* Existence.

It is therefore our intimate, direct experience that Consciousness and Existence are one.

It is our direct experience that we, Consciousness, are Existence, that we *are* what the universe *is*.

In the Christian tradition, this understanding is expressed as, "I and my Father are one." 'I' is Consciousness, that which 'I' truly am. The 'Father' is the Reality of the universe, God.

This expression, "I and my Father are one," is an expression of the fundamental unity of Consciousness and Reality, of the Self with all things.

The fact that in this tradition 'I' has, in most cases, been consistently interpreted as referring to the a single body/mind, and that the 'Father' as a result, has for so many centuries been consistently projected 'outside' at an infinite distance, should not obscure the meaning of the original statement.

Consciousness is present during the appearance of any perception and, when the objective part of the perception disappears, it remains as it always is.

Nothing happens to Consciousness when a perception appears or disappears. It takes the shape of the perception but remains itself, just as a mirror takes on the appearance of an object and yet always remains exactly as it is.

We have no experience of the appearance or disappearance of Consciousness, in spite of the appearance and disappearance of perceptions.

Our experience is that Consciousness endures, that it is permanent. Likewise Reality, Existence, endures.

Of course this statement does not make sense, because it implies that Consciousness and Existence endure in time.

When perception vanishes, time vanishes, because time is the duration between two perceptions. In fact, even during the presence of a perception time is not present, only the *illusion* of time is present. During the so-called interval between two perceptions, not even the illusion of time is present.

So Consciousness and Reality do not endure forever in time. They are ever-present. Always now. They are Eternal. Time, however, *appears* to exist, from time to time, within Consciousness.

Eternity is the term Cezanne uses to refer to this ever-present Reality and he understood the purpose of art as 'giving us a taste' of this Eternity.

He felt that art should lead us to Reality, indicate that which is real, evoke that which is substantial. It should lead us from appearance to Reality. It should point towards the essence of things. And it does so by using the insubstantial, fleeting appearances of sense perceptions, the 'elements of all her (nature's) changes.'

He did not say that art *depicts* Reality any more than literature *describes* it, but rather that it gives us a *taste* of Reality. It takes us to the direct experience, the intimate knowing that Consciousness, what we truly are, *is* the substance of Reality, that there is only one thing, that there is only Being.

William Blake expresses the same understanding when he says, "Every bird that cuts the airy way is an immense world of delight enclosed by the five senses."

He uses the bird as a symbol of nature. He is saying that the Reality of the bird is 'an immense world of delight,' but that its Reality is veiled by the senses. By using the word 'enclosed,' he suggests that the senses somehow limit Reality. They condition its appearance.

It is significant that Blake describes the Reality of nature, of an object, as 'delightful.' Cézanne also says that the Reality of nature, which he calls her 'Eternity,' is experienced as a 'thrill.'

Both Blake and Cézanne are suggesting that inherent in the oneness of Consciousness and Reality is the experience of 'delight,' that the experience is 'thrilling.'

This is in line with Indian philosophy, which describes every experience as an expression of *'nama rupa Sat Chit Ananda.'*

162

'Nama' is 'name.' It is that part of an experience that is supplied or conditioned by thinking. It could be called the concept, the label that the mind uses to frame the experience. It says, "That is a chair." The concept 'chair' is nama.

'Rupa' is 'form.' It is that part of an experience that is supplied by the senses. Each of the senses has their corresponding object in the world. The sense of seeing has its counterpart in the objects of sight. The sense of hearing has its counterpart in the objects of sounds, etc. The senses condition the way Reality appears to us depending on their own characteristics.

'Nama' and 'rupa' together constitute the *appearance* of nature or an object.

If we are to apprehend the real nature of experience, independent of the particular characteristics that are conferred upon it by the mind and senses, we have to denude our experience of that part of it that is supplied by the experiencing apparatus, the instruments of perception, that is the mind and the senses.

As we saw earlier from Cézanne's statement, if we take away that which *appears*, the *objective* aspect of any experience, we are left with the undeniable and yet invisible experience of both Existence or Beingness and Consciousness.

So, in exploring the true nature of experience, we first remove name and form, 'nama' and 'rupa,' the veil of mind and senses in which Reality is 'enclosed.'

This leaves us with the presence of two undeniable facts of experience, Existence and Consciousness, which in Indian philosophy are referred to as 'Sat' and 'chit.'

In every experience there is *something* that is being experienced. That something, whatever it is, is real. It has Being. That is 'sat.'

In every experience there is also *something* that experiences. There is 'I,' Consciousness. That something, whatever it is, is present. It is conscious. That is 'chit.'

From the point of view of the apparent separate entity, we formulate our experience by saying, "I see that." That is, 'I,' Consciousness, sees 'that,' the object or the world. 'Chit' experiences 'Sat.' They are considered to be two things joined by an act of knowing.

However, if we explore our experience carefully, we come to the understanding that Consciousness and Reality are one, that there is no separation between 'I' and 'other', between 'me' and 'you,' between 'me' and the 'world,' between 'Chit' and 'sat.'

The experience of this realisation is known in India as 'Ananda,' which has traditionally been translated as 'bliss.' However, this translation can be misleading. It suggests that the realisation of Oneness is considered to be accompanied by a rare and exotic state. And this in turn initiates the search for an extraordinary experience, for something that is not simply *this*.

'Ananda' is perhaps better translated as Peace or Happiness, or simply Fulfilment. In fact it is very ordinary. It could be described as the absence of agitation or the ease of Being.

Peace and Happiness are normally considered to be a state of the body/mind that result from obtaining a desired object. However, in this formulation from the Indian tradition, Peace and Happiness are understood as being inherent in our true nature, and this accords with both Cézanne and Blake who describe the same experience as a 'thrill' and a 'world of delight.'

When we separate that part of our experience that is imposed or enclosed, as Blake put it, by the mind and senses, by the instruments of perception, Consciousness and Reality are realised to be one.

Their inherent unity is *revealed*. It is not *created*. Peace or Happiness is another name for that experience. It is very natural.

Although *all* objects ultimately come from this experience and are therefore an expression of it, there is a particular category of objects that could be called sacred works of art, that shine with the presence of this understanding and therefore have the power to convey or communicate it directly. They evoke it.

In classical Greece this experience was described as 'Beauty.'

Beauty is not the attribute of an object. It is inherent in the fundamental nature of experience. It is the experience of recognising that Consciousness and Reality are one.

Such sacred works of art stir a deep memory in us. We recognise something in them. In this recognition Consciousness is recognising itself. Consciousness is remembering its own Reality, its own Being.

It looks in the mirror of experience and sees itself. It experiences its own Reality.

Such works of art give us the 'taste of Eternity.'

Consciousness And Being Are One

Identity is inherent in Consciousness.

Consciousness is by nature aware, conscious. That is what it is.

And because it is aware, it is by definition Self-aware, Self-conscious.

Consciousness knows itself at all times, because *knowing* is its nature.

How could something that is itself knowing, not know itself?

Its knowing of itself is not the knowing of *something*.

Its knowing of itself *is* itself.

Knowing is present in every experience.

Consciousness *is* that Knowingness.

This 'knowing' is the illuminating quality in all experience.

The Knowingness of Consciousness is that which illumines all experience.

Consciousness is Self-luminous.

It *is* the light *through* which and *as* which it knows itself.

This Self-knowing is expressed by the term 'I.'

'I' is identity.

Identity is that with which 'I' is one.

Consciousness is one with itself and with all things.

'I am that I am.'

There is nothing present in Consciousness except itself.

Consciousness is empty of objective content, of everything that is not itself.

This emptiness contains all things.

It is a pregnant emptiness.

In its unmanifest state Consciousness knows itself as itself.

When an object appears, it is Consciousness that takes the shape of that object.

Consciousness *knows* an object by *being* that object.

Its *being* an object is one of its modes of knowing itself.

Consciousness can never know an object. It can only know itself.

Its *knowing* itself is its *being* itself.

The *Existence* of an object is its *Being* or 'Isness.'

This Being *is* the knowing of Consciousness knowing itself.

An object derives its *Being* from Consciousness, from 'Amness.'

Being is present in every experience.

Consciousness *is* that Being.

In the knowledge that 'I am,' Consciousness and Being are one.

When this is known, the mind, the body and the world become transparent and luminous.

They shine with Presence, as Presence.

The Fabric Of Self

Prior to the appearance of any object Consciousness is as it is.

This is the condition of unmanifest Consciousness prior to our first experience in the womb, during deep sleep and during the numerous moments between the disappearance of one object and the appearance of the next.

There is nothing to suggest that this will not be the experience of Consciousness after the last appearance of the body at death.

Consciousness is not located in time or space. It is pregnant with the entire universe, including time and space.

Within this vast, pregnant, luminous, empty space of Consciousness, objects appear. Thoughts, images, sensations and perceptions appear.

Initially the 'I am' that is inherent in Consciousness lends itself equally to all appearances.

The 'I am' becomes 'I am That' in the presence of appearances.

Consciousness gives its 'Amness' to all things.

The *Amness* of Self is the *Isness* of things.

Consciousness is *one* with all appearances.

Consciousness knows itself *as* all appearances.

There is Oneness.

At some point, and that moment is always now, Consciousness begins to select some objects over and above others.

Instead of allowing everything to flow freely through itself, as the creator, witness and substance of all appearances, it focuses on some objects in favour of others.

Oneness seems to separate itself into 'Amness' and 'Isness.'

'Amness' becomes 'I' and 'Isness' becomes 'other.'

Consciousness and Being seem to separate.

They appear to become two things.

The innate understanding, 'I am everything,' becomes the belief and the feeling, 'I am some things and not others.'

In order to substantiate this new status of separation, Consciousness bestows its 'ever-presentness' onto a small group of sensations that comprise the body.

The 'I am' which became 'I am That,' 'I am everything,' in the presence of appearances, now becomes 'I am that *particular* thing.' 'I am *something*.'

Consciousness bestows its identity exclusively on the body.

It believes and feels, "I *am* the body."

This belief is continually substantiated by a process of selection, by, 'I like' and 'I don't like.' 'I want' and 'I don't want.'

Consciousness focuses its attention on certain appearances, on certain objects, by trying to hold onto them or by trying to get rid of them.

A web of desire and fear is woven within the vast space of Consciousness, through which some objects pass and in which others are entangled.

This mechanism of likes and dislikes fragments the seamless totality of experience into 'me' and 'not me.'

The objects that are caught in this web become the fabric of the self. The ones that pass through become the world.

In this way the belief and feeling, 'I am the body' is continually substantiated. It becomes dense, solid, sticky, layered.

The return from 'I am something' to 'I am everything,' is simply the loosening of this dense fabric of self.

The tightly woven garment of likes and dislikes in which the self is wrapped becomes looser. It is not so finely woven.

The open space of Consciousness begins to know itself again as a welcoming space in which everything is allowed to pass, as it will, when it will, where it will.

The net of desires and fears is unstitched in this welcoming space and fewer and fewer objects are caught in it.

In the end it is threadbare and what remains of its density is so permeated with space that it no longer has any power to separate anything from anything.

The body returns to its original transparency, open, available, loving and acutely sensitive, but holding onto nothing.

The mind is liberated from the tyranny of a separate self and becomes clear, lively and kind.

The beauty and vibrancy of the world is restored.

The True Dreamer

Experience can be looked at in two ways. One is from the point of view of Consciousness and the other, which is more common, is from the point of view of the apparent separate entity that Consciousness, from time to time, believes and feels itself to be.

To understand how the homogeneous unity of Consciousness is apparently fragmented into separate entities, existing in space and time, we can look at the three states of waking, dreaming and deep sleep.

What are we before we are a body and a mind, before the body and the mind appear?

Do we cease to exist when the body and the mind cease to appear?

And when the body and the mind appear, do we cease to be that which we are before they appeared?

In this moment there is Consciousness and there are appearances. That is, there are these words and whatever else is appearing in this moment, and there is Consciousness, that *to* which, *in* which and, ultimately, *as* which they appear.

The appearances are coming and going all the time.

Imagine that one by one the appearances disappear and are replaced less and less frequently by new ones, until a time comes when there are no appearances at all.

What remains? Simply the Consciousness that was present as the witness of each of the appearances, as they appeared. It is like removing objects from a room, one by one, until only the space of the room remains.

This is the process that is enacted when we fall asleep, when we pass from the waking state to the dream state and from the dream state to deep sleep.

We say, "When we fall asleep…" However, there is in fact no entity that passes from the waking state to the dream state and from the dream state to deep sleep.

Do we have the experience of *someone* who is asleep in deep sleep? No!

Do we have an experience of *someone* who is present as the dreamer of the dream, of *someone* having a dream?

No! That *someone* appears *in* the dream, not *as* the dreamer.

That someone is the subject of the *story* that appears in the dream, but not the *true* subject of the dream. It is not the true dreamer.

That someone appears as one of the *characters* in the dream just like all the other characters.

The apparent *subject* in the dream is in fact one of many *objects* that appear in the dream.

These objects appear to the true dreamer, Consciousness, in which the dream takes place.

As soon as we wake up, we realise that the apparent subject in the dream was in fact *part* of the story. It was an *object* of the true dreamer, Consciousness. We realise that the *apparent* subject in the dream was an *illusory* subject.

However, on waking we immediately and inadvertently fall into another illusion.

We take the subject of the *story* in the waking state, the body/mind, the separate entity, the doer, the feeler, the thinker, the knower, to be the true subject of the waking state, without realising that it is in fact an *object* of the true subject, Consciousness.

The difference between the dream and waking states is that in the dream state the apparent subject is made only of thoughts and images, whereas in the waking state it is made of sensations and perceptions as well.

However, sensing and perceiving are functions of mind, in the same way that thinking and imagining are functions of mind.

The substance of sensing and perceiving, as well as that of thinking and imagining, is mind, and in that sense there is very little difference between the body/mind that appears in the dream state and the body/mind that appears in the waking state.

In the first analysis they are both projections of mind, both made out of mind.

In the final analysis the body/mind that has previously been understood to consist of mind, is further reduced in understanding and is now realised to be a projection of Consciousness, to be made out of Consciousness.

The thoughts and images of the dream state and the thoughts, images, sensations and perceptions of the waking state appear within Consciousness, but do not affect it in any way. How could they? They are made out of it!

One of the thoughts that appear within Consciousness is that of an individual person. This 'individual person' is conceived in many different forms: the experiencer, the doer, the thinker, the enjoyer, the creator, the knower, the sufferer, of all the other objects that appear.

These are the disguises in which the separate entity appears, each one validating and substantiating its apparent existence, like a con-man with several identities.

Upon waking from the dream we discover that the 'individual person' that seemed to be the experiencer *of* the dream was in fact experienced *within* the dream.

However, upon waking we transfer the status of 'experiencer' from the 'individual person' who seems to be present in the *dream* to the 'individual person' who now seems to be present in the *waking state*.

In this way we repeat the mistake and fail to take advantage of the dream experience, which enables us to see that the 'individual person' is in fact an image and a thought in Consciousness, both in the dream *and* in the waking state.

It is for this reason that the waking state is sometimes referred to as the waking dream. The appearance of the separate entity in the waking state is essentially the same as that in the dream state.

In both cases it has no Reality of its own. In both cases its Reality is Consciousness.

To understand the illusion of the waking state we can take the point of view of the dream state.

To understand the illusion of the dream state we can take the point of view of deep sleep.

And to understand the illusion of deep sleep we take the point of view of Consciousness.

That is why the transitions from the waking state to the dream state and from the dream state to deep sleep, and vice versa, are considered in some spiritual traditions to be such significant opportunities for awakening.

In these transitions, that which is illusory in each state is laid bare. And, by the same token, that which is real in each state, that which does not disappear during the transition, is revealed.

At no stage in this process has the essential nature of the body/mind actually changed. It never *becomes* anything other than what it always is – that is, Presence, Consciousness.

There is nobody who passes through any stages. There is simply a flow of thoughts, images, sensations and perceptions, all appearing and disappearing in changeless Presence.

However, our *interpretation* of the nature of the body/mind may change and this new interpretation deeply conditions the way it is experienced, because the body/mind, and the world for that matter, are experienced in accordance with our understanding.

Our experience and its interpretation are co-created within Consciousness.

Consciousness sometimes identifies itself with or imagines itself to be one of the images that it creates within itself during the dreaming or waking state. In this way it imagines itself to be a limited entity, a separate person.

However, at no point does it actually *become* a limited entity or a separate person. It just *imagines* itself to be so, and because it *imagines* this to be so, it *seems* to experience itself as such.

Consciousness *feels* that this is the case and *seems* to experience that it is so, simply because it is the one which creates both the *idea* that it is separate and the apparent *experience* of being separate.

It creates ideas and images as well as sensations and perceptions, and therefore it has the ability to create them consistent with one another.

Thus Consciousness creates within itself the appearance of a separate entity that lives and moves in a separate and independent world, with all the subsequent thoughts, feelings and sensations that are attendant upon this belief.

Consciousness *believes* itself to be that entity and creates experiences within itself that conform to and confirm this belief.

Nothing imposes this activity, this veiling, imagining activity on Consciousness. There is nothing outside Consciousness, so what could there be that imposes this activity?

This veiling activity, this 'imagining-myself-to-be-a-limited-entity' is Consciousness' own activity, its own creativity.

Consciousness is free at every moment to withdraw this projection and to experience itself as it truly is, free, unlimited, Self-luminous, ever-present. And by the same token it is free to create a world that is consistent with this understanding.

We normally consider that the waking state is the most real and normal state, that the dream state is a transitional distortion of the waking state, and that deep sleep is a temporary abyss between states.

We also consider that the 'person,' the individual entity, transitions or travels from one state to another and remains at rest in deep sleep.

From the point of view of the waking state, deep sleep seems to last for a period of time and for that reason it is considered to be a *state*.

A state lasts for a period of time. It begins and ends. We have already seen that there are no objects present in deep sleep and therefore no time.

So deep sleep cannot be said to last for a period of time and therefore cannot be said to be a state.

In deep sleep Consciousness is simply present. It never moves from that 'place.'

There is nobody who is asleep 'there.' There is nobody who wakes up or who transitions from one state to another.

Consciousness is simply present, experiencing its own, unmanifest, ever-present Reality.

The deep sleep state, which is conceived to last a certain amount of time, seems to come and go. However, deep sleep itself is always present.

Whatever is present in deep sleep is equally present in the dreaming and waking states. Deep sleep takes the shape of the dreaming and waking states and is their substance, their underlying Reality.

Imagine the first experience that ever appeared to us as a newborn infant or, even before that, the sensations and perceptions that appeared to us in the womb.

Were we not present as Consciousness before and during that first experience? Must we not have already been present in order to be able to experience that first experience? And has our life since then not simply been a succession of appearances, all appearing to this Consciousness that we are?

And why not go back further than our first experience in the womb? Could it be that whatever experienced the very first appearance that ever occurred, was in fact this very Consciousness that is experiencing these words right now?

Why not? There is no evidence to suggest that it is not the case, and nor is there any evidence to suggest that its opposite, the case for a separate personal Consciousness, is true.

In most cases we presume that Consciousness is limited and personal. Why not give the possibility of Consciousness being universal and unlimited an opportunity?

If there is only one universal Consciousness that is the Reality of all things, then it must already be the case. All that is needed is to align our thoughts, feelings and activities with this possibility and it will be confirmed as such in our actual experience.

The fact that we do not remember this 'first appearance' is not a proof that we, as Consciousness, were not present 'there.' After all, we do not remember being present as Consciousness to witness whatever it was that we were experiencing exactly five days or five years ago. And yet we have no doubt that, at that time, we, this witnessing Consciousness, were the same witnessing Consciousness that is present now, experiencing this current situation.

And before that very first experience, was not Consciousness simply present, simply itself, experiencing itself, because experiencing is its nature? Was it not knowing itself then as it knows itself now, because knowing is its nature?

Was Consciousness not simply present then, Self-luminous, Self-evident, Self-knowing?

And as we have no experience of Consciousness disappearing, appearing or changing, what is there to suggest that the Consciousness that is present 'now' is not exactly the same Consciousness that was present 'then'?

In fact, was that 'then' not this very 'now'? And was that 'there' not this very 'here'?

Of course it does not make sense to say *before that first experience,* because there were, by definition, no ojects present 'then' or 'there,' and without objects there is no time or space.

The primordial space of Consciousness that was present 'before' the appearance of our first experience is a timeless, placeless place.

It was not present 'then' and 'there.' It is present 'here' and 'now.' It is *always* 'here' and 'now.' Not 'here,' a place and 'now,' a time. But rather 'here' and 'now,' this timeless placelessness, this placeless timelessness.

That first experience that took place 'all those billions of years ago,' took place 'here' and 'now' in exactly the same Presence that is seeing these words.

Time and space appear within it. It does not appear within time and space.

What happened to this primordial space of Consciousness when the first object, the first experience, appeared?

Did anything happen to it?

Did it move or change?

Did we ever experience its appearance or disappearance?

Is it possible to conceive of something that was present before it, which was not itself Consciousness?

And is this primordial space of Consciousness that was present to witness the first experience we ever had or that ever was, not exactly the same empty space of Consciousness that is present during deep sleep?

Is it not present now?

Will it change when the last object leaves it on death?

Does it change or disappear when the first image of a dream appears in it on making the transition from deep sleep to the dream state?

In each case Consciousness always simply remains as it is.

Reality is one solid seamless indivisible substance, made out of luminosity, transparency, Knowingness, Beingness.

In deep sleep Consciousness abides in and as itself. The entire universe and all universes are enfolded within it, ready to take shape at any moment but as yet unmanifest.

With the appearance of the first image or thought, the dream state begins. Consciousness takes the shape of these first images and thoughts. It becomes these images and thoughts and yet, at the same time, remains itself.

It expresses itself and witnesses itself simultaneously in and as these images and thoughts.

With the appearance of these images and thoughts, the illusion of time is created, but the illusion of space is still not present.

It is the appearance of sensations and perceptions that affect the transition from the dream state to the waking state, and with the appearance of sensations and perceptions comes the illusion of space.

It is true that an image of space appears in the dream state, but on waking we realise that the dream actually took place only in time, not in space.

At no stage in this process does Consciousness become anything other than what it always already is.

At no stage in this process does anything appear outside Consciousness or separate from Consciousness.

In the dream state Consciousness takes the shape of thoughts and images and at this moment gives birth to the dream world, which contains the dimension of time. It is a mono-dimensional world.

In fact there is never any *actual* experience of time and space themselves. With the birth of the mind – that is, with the appearance of thinking and imagining within Consciousness – the illusion of time is imposed on Reality.

And with the birth of the world – that is, with the appearance of sensing and perceiving – the illusion of space is imposed on Reality.

Divested of mind and senses, divested of name and form, the apparent continuum of time and space is revealed to be what in fact it always is, the ever-presence of Consciousness.

In the waking state Consciousness takes the shape of sensations and perceptions as well as thoughts and images, and at this moment gives birth to the waking world, which contains the dimensions of space as well as that of time. It is a four-dimensional world.

Consciousness projects the dream world within itself through the functions of thinking and imagining.

Consciousness projects the waking world within itself through the functions of sensing and perceiving, as well as thinking and imagining.

In deep sleep there is no projection and therefore no time or space. There is no world.

There is simply Presence and that Presence is this Presence.

The Here And Now Of Presence

All experience takes place *here*.

This *here* is not a physical space. It is the space of Consciousness in which all experiences, including the apparent experience of space, takes place.

A distant sound takes place *here*.

The thought that subsequently conceives that sound to be at a distance from the perceiving Consciousness takes place in the same space as the sound itself. It takes place *here*.

The chair on 'the other side of the room' is perceived *here*, in exactly the same place as the sound and the thought, at no distance from Consciousness.

All bodily sensations take place in the same placeless place, which is *here*.

It is not that Consciousness is present *everywhere*. It is that *everywhere* is present *here*.

This *here* is not a location inside the body. The body is a sensation inside this *here*, inside Presence.

Once it is understood and felt that everything takes place 'here,' 'inside' Consciousness, the idea that experiences take place 'there' or 'outside' vanishes.

However, the idea of 'here' and 'inside' need their opposite, 'there' and 'outside,' to have any meaning.

Therefore, when the 'there' and the 'outside' vanish, the 'here' and the 'inside' also collapse.

The 'here' and the 'inside' are just intermediary steps to relieve Consciousness of the idea and the subsequent feeling that there is something 'there' and 'outside,' at a distance from itself.

Once this is seen clearly, the 'here' and the 'inside' can also be abandoned and Consciousness is left on its own, without attributes, to shine in and as itself, prior to time and place.

When the 'there' is withdrawn the 'here' is revealed. When the 'here' is dissolved, Consciousness shines as it is.

All experience takes place *now*.

All memories of the past take place *now*.

All thoughts about the future take place *now*.

This *now* does not last in time. All time lasts in it.

However, the 'now' cannot exist without the idea of a 'then,' a past or a future. Therefore the past and the future are reduced, in understanding, to the present and then the present, which cannot stand alone, is merged into Consciousness.

The 'here' of space and the 'now' of time are revealed as the same placeless, timeless presence of Consciousness.

This placeless, timeless Presence is the transparent, homogeneous, substantial, ever-present Reality of experience *within* which and ultimately *as* which the fleeting, insubstantial and intermittent experiences that we call the body, the mind and the world appear like waves.

Imagine that one wall of the room we are sitting in is composed entirely of mirror.

The image that appears in the mirror will be identical to the room in which we are sitting. The space that appears in the mirror will appear identical to the space that appears in the room.

However, when we reach out our hand and try to touch the physical objects or the space that appear in the mirror we touch only the mirror, not the objects or the space.

Although there is an illusion of space in the mirror, in fact everything that appears in the mirror appears at the same distance from it – that is, at no distance at all.

Nothing is closer to the mirror than anything else.

Consciousness is like a three-dimensional mirror in which everything appears.

Everything that appears in the mirror of Consciousness is at the same distance from it, and that is no distance at all.

Whatever we touch, we touch only Presence.

Whatever we perceive, we perceive only Presence.

Whatever we experience, we, this Presence, only ever experience our Self.

Every experience is *one* with Presence.

Every experience *is* Presence.

Consciousness Is Self-Luminous

The mirror of Consciousness is the screen on which everything is experienced and, at the same time, it is that which experiences everything.

The image that appears in the mirror is made only of mirror. Whatever appears in Consciousness is made only of Consciousness.

When an object appears it seems to colour the mirror and this colouring of the mirror seems to give the mirror object-like qualities.

When the image vanishes the mirror again becomes the transparent mirror. In fact it was always only this.

Consciousness is transparent and cannot be seen as an object, in the same way that the glass out of which the mirror is made cannot be seen unless an object is being reflected in it.

When an object is present, whether that object is a thought, a sensation or a perception, the presence of the object enables us to perceive Consciousness – that is, it enables Consciousness to perceive itself, to experience itself.

In fact Consciousness is always perceiving itself, in the presence and in the absence of an object.

Even if we do not realise it, when we experience an object – that is, when an object appears in Consciousness – it is Consciousness that is experiencing itself *as* that apparent object. An object is one of Consciousness' modes of Self-knowing.

We could say that the transparent medium of Consciousness is coloured by the appearance of an object.

It is the colour in the glass that enables us to see the glass. Without the colour, the glass would be completely transparent and therefore invisible.

This metaphor is helpful in that it allows us to understand that when an object is present, it is only Consciousness that is experiencing itself. However, like all metaphors, it is limited.

Unlike the mirror or the transparent glass, Consciousness is conscious. It perceives. It experiences itself all the time, whether or not objects are present.

So Consciousness does not need a knower outside of itself in order to be known. Nor does it need the presence of an object to know itself. It does not need a body or a mind in order to know itself.

Consciousness knows itself *before* it knows anything else, and when it knows *something*, whether that 'something' is an object of the body, mind or world, it is still only knowing itself, *as* that something.

Consciousness knows itself prior to the appearance of the body/ mind. This knowledge is continuous and ever-present. Objects do not obscure it or veil it. They reveal it. More than that they shine with that very knowledge.

A more accurate metaphor would be that of a limitless space.

Every part of this space is conscious, sensitive, aware.

The nature of this space is to be conscious. It cannot turn off this awareness.

Imagine that within this limitless, knowing space, several holographic images, each of a different house, are projected. Each house is like a separate body/mind.

Does this limitless space change in any way when the images of the hologram are projected within it?

What happens to the space when some of the images of the houses are withdrawn and when new ones appear?

Is the space that appears within the walls of the apparent houses limited by those walls?

Is it not the same space inside, outside and within the walls themselves?

Is there ever any separation or division within this space?

Is this space ever anything other than itself?

Is there anywhere in this image where the space is not present?

Is the appearance of the houses made out of anything other than the space in which it appears?

Is there any substance present, out of which the houses could be made, other than the space itself?

When the houses appear or disappear, does the space become anything other than what it already is?

Do the houses have any other reality that is other than or apart from the space itself?

When the space 'knows' the houses does it know anything other than itself?

For the space, is not the act of *being* the house, the same act as *knowing* the house?

Does not this knowing space know itself in and as the current experience of the house and, at the same time, is it not always present, obvious, illuminating itself, knowing itself?

If we now proceed from the metaphor of limitless space to our own intimate, immediate and direct experience of our Self, of Consciousness, and from the image of the houses to our actual experience of the cluster of sensations that we call the body, which appears within this Consciousness, what do we find?

What is our actual experience of the body?

If we ask ourselves all the same questions as in the metaphor above, not theoretically but moment by moment in our actual felt, lived experience, do we not find that, like the houses, our actual experience of the body is weightless, transparent, luminous, spacious, open, welcoming, without limits or borders, without definition, without location, all embracing and, at the same time, revealing itself to itself, astonishing itself, delighting itself, in and as every detail and nuance of this moment, and this moment and this moment?

Consciousness Only Knows Itself

*"Never did eye see the sun unless it had first become sun-like
and never can the soul have vision of the First Beauty
unless itself be beautiful."*

PLOTINUS

Consciousness cannot know an object.

Such an object would have to be outside or separate from itself.

How could Consciousness know something that was outside or separate from itself? How would it make contact with such an object?

Consciousness knows a thing by being that thing. That is its mode of knowing anything.

To know an object Consciousness has first to transform that object into itself. The object is transformed into the substance of Consciousness, in order to be known *by* Consciousness, *as* Consciousness.

However, that is written for the mind that insists that objects exist in their own right, outside Consciousness.

In fact no such thing happens. The object is never outside Consciousness in the first place and therefore there is no question of taking it in or transforming it.

Rather, Consciousness takes the shape of the object, of the current experience, from moment to moment, whilst always remaining exactly as it is.

As the water in the ocean rises and swells into the shape of a wave, flows for a while and then falls back into the ocean, without ever for

192

a moment being anything other than water, so every object, every experience, arises within Consciousness, takes its unique shape, does its unique thing, and then offers back its name and form to the ocean of Presence, which abides in and as itself, before taking the shape of the next wave.

The wave gives water a name and a form. When the wave vanishes, only name and form vanish. Water remains as it always is.

The object does not dissolve in Consciousness. It is always only Consciousness. There is nothing to dissolve.

There is no part of the object that is not Consciousness and Consciousness cannot dissolve. Into what would it dissolve?

The Reality of whatever is present when an object is present, is Consciousness, and that Reality is ever-present.

Nothing ever disappears. Only names and forms are continually transformed.

There is a tombstone in a graveyard in Krakow on which every letter of the alphabet is carved. Everyone who has ever lived is remembered there.

That which truly lives is acknowledged there, eternally.

One tomb, many names.

One womb, many forms.

Wherever we look we see only the face of God.

God sees herself in all things.

Consciousness Is Freedom Itself

I often hear it said that there is nothing one can do with the thinking mind to achieve enlightenment. Is this so?

The simple answer is, "Yes, but...."

The thinking mind is a series of abstract concepts with which we, as a culture, have agreed by common consent to represent our experience so as to enable us to communicate.

The language of the mind is a code. It converts direct experience into a currency that can be used and exchanged for the practical purposes of functioning at the level of the mind, body and world.

The language of the mind does not deliver the object that it represents. It indicates it.

However, we forget this and take the mind's formulations as true descriptions of our experience. We say, "I see the car," and in doing so, truly believe and feel that there is an 'I,' an entity, in 'here,' that does something called 'seeing' in relation to an object 'out there,' the car, thereby enabling the 'I' to experience 'it.'

There is nothing wrong with this as long as it is understood to be a provisional formulation that enables a particular aspect of life to take place. It is a way of seeing and talking that enables a certain level of functioning in the world and, as such, it has its legitimate place.

However, it is only when we take such a statement as a *description* of our actual experience, as a description of Reality, that the confusion begins.

The statement, "I see the car," does not represent the true nature of the actual *experience* of seeing the car. For this reason the non-dual teaching, whose aim and purpose is to understand and reveal the true nature of experience, is often suspicious, to the point of rejection, of the mind's role in the unveiling of Reality.

"After all," the argument goes, "it is the dualistic nature of the thinking mind that created the problem in the first place. Why would we rely on the same deceptive instrument to alleviate it?"

Imagine that a man is sitting in a room looking at himself in a mirror on the opposite wall. After a while the man begins to construct an edifice between himself and the mirror that obscures his reflection until he is no longer able to see himself.

In this image the man represents Consciousness, the mirror represents the apparently objective world of experience and the edifice represents the dualistic concepts of the mind.

It is the edifice of ideas that seems to prevent Consciousness from knowing itself knowingly, from perceiving itself, just as it is the edifice that prevents the man from seeing himself in the mirror.

It is true therefore that anything the man adds on to this edifice will only further obscure his reflection. And that is the 'Yes...' part of the answer.

However, the man can deconstruct the edifice. In fact he is well placed to do so because he built it. He knows exactly how it was constructed and, by the same token, exactly how to deconstruct it.

The deconstruction of the edifice is simply the investigation of the mind's belief that 'I' is a separate, personal entity, and the exploration of the feeling that 'I' is the body or is located *in* the body.

A belief is an idea that we *think* is true. A fact is an idea that we *know* is true. The 'dismantling of the edifice' is the process by which we distinguish between the two, between a belief and a fact.

Imagine that we think that two plus two equals five, that we *think* it is a fact. At some point we begin to doubt this 'fact,' either through intuition, or because we read or hear something to the effect that two plus two may not equal five. A seed of doubt is planted in our minds.

The presence of a doubt indicates, by definition, the presence of a belief underneath it. Belief and doubt always come together. If a thought represents a fact, we know it, we do not believe it. And if we know it we do not doubt it. If we doubt it we do not know it. And if we do not know it, it is a belief and not a fact.

The 'dismantling of the edifice,' the dismantling of that which prevents the man from seeing himself in the mirror, of that which prevents Consciousness from knowing itself knowingly, is, at the level of the mind, the investigation of our thoughts. Are they facts or are they beliefs?

A thorough investigation of our ideas reveals most of them to be beliefs rather than facts.

We begin to explore our ideas. We no longer *know* that two plus two equals five. We realise that we *think* it equals five, we *believe* it equals five, but we are not sure. There is some doubt. The apparent fact has been reduced to a belief through investigation.

On further investigation we discover that two plus two equals four, not five. At this point the belief vanishes spontaneously and instantaneously. However, it is still possible for the idea 'two plus two equals five' to occur. The belief has vanished but the idea may remain.

So the investigation into the nature of our experience involves the reduction, in our understanding, of apparent facts to beliefs and the subsequent reduction of beliefs to ideas.

An idea by itself, an idea that has not yet become a belief, is innocuous. It cannot separate anything from anything. Whether we choose to entertain such an idea is entirely up to us. For instance, we may choose to take the thought 'two plus two equals five' in order to understand a child's mind and teach him or her arithmetic.

Likewise we may choose to think that we are a separate person in order to enjoy and suffer the rich tapestry of thoughts, feelings, sensations, emotions, perceptions, images and activities that result from this idea. That is our freedom, Consciousness' freedom.

It is the freedom that Consciousness has from moment to moment: to create the idea that it is a separate, personal entity, to believe that idea, to forget that it has chosen to believe it and therefore consider it a fact, to explore the fact and rediscover that it is a belief, to stop believing it and realise again that it is simply an idea, and is, as such, one of many possible modes of being that Consciousness chooses from moment to moment, out of its own freedom.

There is nothing wrong with the idea of a separate personal entity. However, the exclusive association of Consciousness with that idea is problematic. In this case the *idea* of the separate entity is turned into the *belief* that, "I *am* that separate entity."

The upgrading of the idea to a belief, and subsequently of the belief to an apparent fact, is discovered on investigation to be the sole cause of psychological suffering.

However Consciousness is free to do this, just as it is free to stop doing it. Consciousness is freedom itself. It is free to forget and free to remember.

It is true that the thought that 'two plus two equals five' arises in the same Consciousness as the idea that 'two plus two equals four.' As such both are equally expressions of Consciousness.

However, it would be simplistic to say that both thoughts are equally true, simply because they both appear in and are ultimately made out of the same Consciousness.

From the ultimate point of view, it is true that both ideas are equal, but as soon as we are on the relative level, it is disingenuous to say so.

The question as to whether there is anything one can do with the thinking mind to achieve enlightenment gives credence to the idea of an individual entity, which may or may not have the capacity to do something. Implicit in the idea of such an entity is the presumption that this entity is itself a doer. That entity cannot therefore legitimately say that there is nothing to do. It is already the doer.

It would be more honest for that apparent entity to explore its own nature. In this way we avoid superimposing an idea that is true at the absolute level, where it is clearly seen that there is nothing to do and that there are no separate entities, onto the relative level, where the belief and feeling in the reality of the separate entity are at least provisionally accepted.

In this issue of there being nothing to do, the levels of Consciousness and mind are often confused. The absolute truths of one are used to justify the relative truths of the other. This, incidentally, is one of the ways that ego (that is, Consciousness-pretending-to-be-a-separate-entity) perpetuates itself. It is one of its safer refuges.

Once we are using the mind we are knowingly or unknowingly agreeing, at least temporarily, to its concepts and therefore its limitations.

We take a step down, so to speak, from the ultimate level of Consciousness and agree to discuss the undiscussable, to think about the unthinkable, to point towards that which cannot be seen or named.

This is why Ramana Maharshi was often silent when asked a question. The highest answer to a question about the nature of Reality or the Self is always Reality or the Self itself, and this cannot be spoken of. So he would just remain silent.

However, there were many who could not receive the subtlety of this answer, and for those he would tone down the frequency of his answer, so to speak, so that it would resonate with their understanding.

The teacher, for instance, might *appear* to condone the existence of a separate entity in his answer, if this was deemed necessary to help the student take a step towards understanding.

However, it would be simplistic to suggest that in this case the teacher was not speaking the truth, or that his teaching was somehow limited.

It is a counterpart to, and as simplistic as thinking that one who simply answers every question with, "Everything is Consciousness and therefore everything is the same" is necessarily coming from the ultimate understanding.

It is the deep understanding from which the teaching comes, rather than the 'political correctness' of the words themselves that indicates the truth of the teaching. And there is a great freedom of expression that is available to a true teacher, which will cover a wide range of formulations, including ones that may sometimes seem to contradict one another.

It is true that anything said in words, anything the mind produces, has a level of relativity to it, and hence a degree of untruth, a lack of completeness. However, what is important is the deep understanding behind the words.

If the words speak a relative truth and yet come from true understanding beyond the mind, it is ultimately the truth of this understanding that is transmitted.

And likewise if the 'absolute truth' is spoken by one who is parroting the truth and yet does not come from true understanding, the answer will lack depth, and that will be transmitted.

If Consciousness is capable of building the edifice of conceptual thinking that apparently divides itself from itself, then it is by definition capable of dismantling that edifice.

We are deceiving ourselves if we wash a veneer of 'unknowing' over deeply held beliefs and prejudices, or a veneer of 'There is only one Consciousness' over feelings that 'I' *am* this body or am *in* this body.

Once we have explored our beliefs thoroughly, we discover that the ideas, 'I am a separate entity' and 'The world is outside myself,' are not substantiated by experience.

Once we have understood that there is no experiential evidence to suggest that Consciousness, which is seeing these words, is either personal or limited, or that it is an object, a crisis takes place. We may *know* that we are not a separate entity but we still *feel* that we are a separate 'me' located inside a body.

As a result we start to explore not only the *belief* that I am a separate entity, a body/mind, but the *feeling* that I am such.

This is undertaken through a direct exploration of feelings and bodily sensations and bypasses the conceptual faculties of the mind.

It is an experiential exploration rather than a rational investigation into the nature of separation, and as such little can be said about it in rational terms, although some hints may be given. It is for this reason that not much is said in this book about this exploration at the level of the body.

However, this is not to suggest that this deeper exploration into the nature of separation, is not, in most cases, required in order to be stable in Peace and Happiness.

In fact, in some ways, it could be said that the rational investigation at the level of beliefs and ideas is a prelude to the deeper exploration of the sense of separation at the level of the body.

The *belief* in separation is the tip of the iceberg. The vast majority of the iceberg remains hidden under water in the murky realms of feelings and bodily sensations.

Many of us 'know' that we are unlimited but we *feel* limited. We may understand the theory of non-duality but in the privacy of our hearts the fire of longing still burns.

It is for this reason that some people who have been on a spiritual path for many decades still feel a sense of separation and longing, a sense that something is missing, a lack of fulfilment.

For most people who are deeply interested in the nature of experience, this contradiction is intolerable and precipitates a deeper exploration at the level of feelings and sensations.

The initial enquiry into the nature of experience could be called the Path of Discrimination. It leads to the realisation that, 'I am nothing.'

The deeper exploration at the level of the body and the world could be called the Path of Love. It leads to the realisation that, 'I am everything.'

In the Path of Discrimination we discover what we are not.

In the Path of Love we discover what we are.

This discovery is a moment by moment revelation. It cannot be crystallised in words.

It is the true unknowing in which nothing is known but everything is embraced.

It Has Always Been So

Every experience, every appearance, is a wave on the ever-present ocean of Presence.

If we look at the waves they change from moment to moment.

If we look at the water, the water itself never changes.

The water never comes and goes.

Nothing ever happens to the water itself.

The same is true of experience.

Where does one appearance go when the next one appears?

And what happens to the substance out of which the first appearance was made, when that appearance disappears?

How could that substance disappear?

How could something become nothing?

And where did the substance from which the first appearance was made, come from?

Can nothing become something?

Do we experience a single flow of events or a succession of momentary events?

If there is a single flow, how do we account for the appearance and disappearance of anything?

The *flow* of a river always changes shape, but the *substance* of a river never disappears.

And if our experience is a succession of moments, how long is a moment?

How long is the interval between these moments and what is it made of?

If it is made of something, that something would itself be an appearance, and not therefore an interval *between* appearances.

If it was made of nothing, it would be nothing. It would not be. It would not have Existence.

Does this interval *appear* between appearances and does it *disappear* during the existence of an appearance?

If it appears and disappears it must be an appearance, and if it is not an appearance and yet is present, it must be ever-present.

Experience is like an image on a TV screen. Appearances come and go, but in fact the appearance of the image is nothing but the screen and the screen does not come and go.

Whatever goes into the make of one appearance on the screen is exactly the same thing that goes into the make of the next.

The interval between appearances is not an interval. It is the screen. And the screen is the permanent substance of every appearance.

The screen never appears or disappears. It does not come and go.

There are not numerous independent images that come and go. There is one screen that from time to time takes the appearance of a flow of images. The appearances seem to move and flow, but the screen never moves or flows.

Nor does the screen ever vanish. It does not *become* anything other than itself, even when it appears as a house, a field or a car. It is always only itself.

The red pixel that went into the make of the car on the screen remains exactly the same pixel in the next image of a strawberry.

The substance of every appearance is the screen, just as the substance of every experience is Presence.

We do not experience a multitude of moments. We experience one ever-present Now. And this ever-present Now is coloured from time to time with apparent objectivity.

The refraction of the screen into an apparent multiplicity of objects is in appearance only. We are in fact always seeing the screen. There is in fact only ever one thing that is present and the substance of that thing is only the screen.

Likewise, in our experience, diversity is in appearance only. At any moment of apparently objective experience there is in fact only one experience present.

When we have reduced the multiplicity of things, in understanding, to one thing, we can further reduce that 'one thing' into our Self, the permanent background and substance of all things.

This discovery does not *make* it so but rather *reveals* that it has always been so.

Sameness And Oneness

If everything is one Consciousness, do ideas of right and wrong have any relevance?

The question is already the answer.

Right there in the question itself is the confusion that leads to the question and, by the same token, the answer is implied in it. It is the result of a misunderstanding of levels.

If we deeply feel and think that everything is an expression of one Consciousness, of one Reality, then the actions and behaviour that spring from that feeling and thought will, by definition, be in line with it.

Each action will be in harmony with the one Reality simply because it proceeds from that, not just in theory, but in thought and feeling.

It is our experience that if we *feel* hateful, we *act* hatefully. If we *feel* loving, we *act* lovingly. Likewise, if we truly feel that everything and everyone is an expression of the same one Reality that we ourselves are, we will act accordingly and will quite literally behave towards others as we would behave towards ourselves.

That does not mean we will always have a sweet smile on our face. We will often come across situations where the understanding that everything is an expression of one Reality is not present, and our subsequent actions will be appropriate to that situation. In fact they arise *out of* that situation. Nevertheless, whatever the shape of that action, it will come from the feeling of the essential oneness of all things.

This is not to suggest that any action that does not come from the feeling of oneness is somehow not an expression of that oneness. It absolutely is. Everything, everything is an expression of that one-ness. Ignorance and wisdom alike.

Every thought, however beautiful or ugly it may be, arises in the same presence of Consciousness, which is its very substance.

However, this fact does not magically turn ignorance into wisdom. It does not mean that, at a relative level, unloving behaviour is the same as loving behaviour. All thoughts are equal in the sense that they are all ultimately expressions of the same Reality. Their *substance* is the same but their objective *content* is not.

If we see a rope and think that it is a snake we will act appropriately and try to catch it, avoid it or kill it. If we see that it is a rope, we just walk by.

Both the sight of the rope and the sight of the apparent snake, both the thought of the rope and the thought of the apparent snake, appear in Consciousness.

The substance of each perception and each thought is the same that is, Consciousness. However, that does not mean that both thoughts are true at the level of mind. It is true that it is a rope. It is not true that it is a snake.

Likewise, the behaviour that follows from seeing the rope or seeing the snake is very different. When we see the rope, we just walk by. When we think we see the snake, fear is born and most of our subsequent thoughts, feelings and activities are governed by this fear.

If we experience Consciousness everywhere, we do not experience objects, although of course we experience apparent objects.

In fact we only ever experience Consciousness. That is, Consciousness only ever experiences itself. So when it is said, 'If we experience Consciousness everywhere…' it means, 'If we *knowingly* experience Consciousness everywhere…'

If we think we experience objects, we are not experiencing Consciousness, knowingly.

If we think we see a snake, we are not seeing the rope, knowingly.

The rope and the snake are the same in substance, but they are different, as appearance.

To experience separate objects is not to experience Consciousness, knowingly. To experience Consciousness knowingly is not to experience objects.

We cannot claim to be experiencing objects and Consciousness at the same time, any more than we can claim to see the rope and the snake at the same time.

Of course when we see that everything is Consciousness, that everything is one Reality, we continue to see *apparent* objects.

However, we cannot think that we see the snake and claim to see the rope at the same time. They are mutually exclusive positions. Seeing the rope is synonymous with no longer seeing the snake. Once we see the rope we can still see the *appearance* of the snake, but we know that it is a rope.

Maya still dances, but it is a dance of love not seduction.

Similarly, if we know deeply that everything is an expression of Consciousness, that everything *is* Consciousness, we see Consciousness everywhere.

As a result we no longer believe the divisive, dualistic concepts of the mind. We no longer believe in good and bad as absolute realities. However, that does not mean that they cease to appear at the level of the mind or that they are not appropriate at that level.

Similarly, if we see good and bad as absolute realities, if we believe in them, we are not seeing everything as one Reality. Once we have labelled something as good or bad, we are already committed to mind, to its dualistic concepts.

If we see everything as an expression of one Reality, we are taking our stand at a place that is prior to the mind, prior to good and bad, right and wrong. We have not yet divided our experience with the mind although the mind is still available for use when appropriate.

However, if we do not see and feel that everything is an expression of one Reality, then we are by definition seeing our experience, seeing the one Reality, through the dualistic filter of the mind, and opposites, good and bad, right and wrong, are inherent at that level. That is what mind is. There is nothing wrong with that, but we should at least be clear about the nature of our ideas.

The same goes for beauty and ugliness. At the level of the mind, beauty and ugliness exist. At the level of Consciousness they do not.

Beauty does not have a purpose. It is already the fulfilment of any purpose.

However, from the level of the mind, its purpose could be said to draw attention to the absolute Beauty that is the substance of *all* things.

To say that there are no beautiful or ugly objects is disingenuous. It is to superimpose the apparent understanding that everything is one Consciousness and that there are therefore no objects onto the deeply held belief and feeling that there are objects.

Once we see objects, we are in duality. And once we are in duality, there is good and bad, right and wrong, beauty and ugliness.

However, if we are looking from the point of view of Consciousness, then there are no objects and therefore no good and bad, right and wrong, beauty or ugliness.

Neither the position of Consciousness nor the position of the mind is problematic. In fact both are necessary for the healthy functioning of the apparent individual in the apparent world.

However, it is problematic is to pretend that at the level of mind there is no diversity, no difference, no values, that one thing is as good as another.

It is disingenuous to appropriate the understanding that is true from the point of view that there is only one Reality, and to pretend that it holds true at a level where we have already denied that very Reality, by dividing it up into separate entities.

That is the confusion between sameness and Oneness.

This is one of the limitations of teachings that only present us with statements of the absolute truth. Whilst they may be true, these statements are often appropriated by the mind as a belief, and laid as a thin veneer on top of already existing beliefs, which in fact simply get buried deeper as a result.

Consciousness liberates itself with clarity and honesty, not with the superimposition of beliefs and dogma.

Sooner or later Consciousness comes to see the difference between its own openness, its own Presence, which welcomes all things into itself with benevolent indifference, and a mind which, by definition, sees differences and yet has imposed on itself a strait-jacket of 'non-judging.'

Such 'non-judging' comes from fear and confusion. It is not the true, benevolent indifference of Presence.

A Knowing Space

If it is acknowledged that enlightenment is a non-experience and cannot be framed within language, why is it necessary to go to such lengths to describe the understanding?

It is not Understanding, which can only be formulated in the most approximate terms, that is being described here. Rather it is *misunderstanding* that is being exposed.

Understanding is *revealed* by thought, not *explained* by it.

In fact, it is the *ending* of thought that reveals Understanding, and a process of thinking is just one of the ways that thought is brought to an end.

To begin with, this Understanding, which is not an objective knowing, is revealed when thought comes to an end. Later it is realised to be present *during* thought itself.

It is the origin and substance of thought, not just its destiny.

With one exception, Reality cannot be touched by the mind, although the mind is always shining with its light, in the same way that the moon shines with the sun's light.

That exception is the thought about Reality itself. When we think about the nature of Reality, the mind comes to its own limit, because Reality is beyond the abstract concepts of the mind and therefore has no objective characteristics. It is like a man who runs towards a precipice and comes to the edge. If he proceeds he plunges into the void and dies.

The thought that seeks Reality comes to its own limit and plunges into Reality itself. It dies in that which it was seeking, and its dissolution is the revelation of that ever-present Reality.

Even misunderstandings shine with the light of Truth, the light of Consciousness, although they appear to obscure it.

Many people have profound spiritual experiences at some stage in their lives, often early on. By 'profound spiritual experience' is simply meant a glimpse of Truth, of Reality, a moment when Consciousness recognises its own oneness with Reality. It is not really an experience in the ordinary sense of the word because it has no objective qualities.

This non-objective experience has an impact on the body/mind and is usually described in terms of some sort of release or expansion. This release or expansion is the impact that a glimpse of Truth has on the body/mind. It is the packaging, so to speak.

However, the essence of the experience, a moment of Consciousness knowing itself knowingly, is colourless and transparent, and therefore cannot be remembered.

We do, however, remember the impact of this non-objective experience at the level of the body and the mind. This impact is often confused with the non-objective experience of Consciousness knowing itself and, as a result, these states of the body/mind become the object of intense seeking that sometimes lasts a whole lifetime.

However, these states, like all states, come and go. They are by nature impermanent, so by seeking them Consciousness is condemning itself to an endless cycle of becoming, in which the failure to secure Happiness is intrinsic.

It tries over and over again to reproduce the experience, which it construes as having taken place in the body or the mind at a certain time in the past.

However, the experience that it is looking for is the experience of its own Self, its own ever-present Reality, which is lying behind and within every experience, including the experience of seeking itself.

The experience that Consciousness is looking for is *prior* to the body and the mind, not prior in time and space, but prior to their arising moment by moment.

Consciousness is like the space that is present before a house is built, except that it is a Self-knowing space.

When the house is built, the walls of the house appear to condition the space in which it is built, but when the house is demolished, we realise that the space in fact never changed, that it was never in fact limited by the house.

Nothing ever happens to the space itself.

We think we enter the house but we do not. We enter the space that appears to have the name and the shape of the house.

The only difference here, in this Self-knowing space of Consciousness, is that no one is entering or leaving the space. The space is a Self-conscious space. It is a space that is 'knowing.' It knows itself.

Imagine that the space in which the house is built is also a knowing space. Before the house is built, this space is aware of itself as space. When the house is built it has the option either to continue being aware of itself exactly as it still is and always has been, or to look at the shape of the walls and to impose their limitations on its own unlimitedness.

When the house is demolished, the space does not go anywhere. It does not unite with anything. It stays exactly as it always was and is.

The house is the body/mind. The experience of a thought, sensation or perception coming to an end is the experience of the demolition of the house. The space recognises itself as space.

Consciousness recognises itself as Consciousness. That is the experience of Love, Humour, Beauty, Understanding.

At some stage the house does not need to be demolished for the space to continue knowing itself as space.

It knows itself as space during the presence *and* the absence of the house. It becomes obvious that the house does not really separate the space outside from the space inside, that the space that appears to be contained *within* the house is in fact exactly the same space that *contains* the house.

In exactly the same way, every time we experience Love, Humour, Beauty, Understanding, Consciousness is experiencing itself knowingly.

When the body/mind returns, it returns saturated with the afterglow of this transparent experience. It is permeated with the peace of Presence.

This is the same experience as awaking from deep sleep. On waking, the body/mind reappears in Presence, saturated with the peace of deep sleep, which is none other than the peace of our true nature.

Exposing the wrong formulations of our experience, the misunderstandings, relieves Consciousness of the relentless search for itself in the realm of the body, mind and world.

It relieves Consciousness of the search for itself as an object.

As soon as Consciousness releases itself in this way, it finds that it is always present, that its own Presence is always here shining and always has been.

Consciousness is in the looking, not in the looked for.

Consciousness sees itself shining within itself, the open, empty, self-luminous Presence welcoming itself back to itself, in the place where it never left.

And now, when it looks back at the old objects that seemed to veil itself from itself, it sees them shining in and as itself, separating nothing from nothing, just as the walls of the house appeared to separate the space inside from the space outside, but in fact separated nothing from nothing.

Consciousness Peace 'I'

"That which is not present in deep, dreamless sleep is not real."
RAMANA MAHARSHI

Taking our stand as the witness establishes the fact that Consciousness is independent of objects and present throughout their appearance.

Consciousness is present and, by definition, conscious. That is what it is and that is our experience in this moment.

How would it be possible for whatever is seeing these words to see them, if it was not conscious?

When no objects are present, such as in deep sleep, this Consciousness is, by definition, still conscious. It is conscious of itself, but not of objects. That is why it is called Self-luminous and Self-knowing.

It both illumines and knows itself at the same time, all the time.

Deep sleep is the experience of Consciousness knowing its own luminous Self.

What else is present in the experience of deep sleep?

Peace and myself.

Peace is not an objective experience. It is simply the presence of Consciousness without an object. That is why it is peaceful!

It is this experience of Peace that we look forward to when we go to sleep. And it is this experience that enables the body and the mind to reappear refreshed in the morning.

The body/mind reappears in the morning, saturated with the peace from which it arises.

Likewise 'myself,' my real Self, not the separate entity that appears as an object of thought or feeling from time to time, but the Self that I have always been and always am, is present in deep sleep.

In fact it is not quite right to say that it is present in deep sleep, because that implies that it is some kind of an object that exists *in* deep sleep. It is more accurate to say that 'I,' my Self, *am* deep sleep.

Deep sleep is the experience of Consciousness, Peace and my Self simultaneously. That is our own direct, intimate and immediate experience.

There are no objects in deep sleep and therefore no boundaries, so Consciousness, Peace and my Self are identical.

When the first object, usually a dream, appears after deep sleep, it does not appear as an object coming *into* this presence of 'Consciousness-Peace-I.' Where would it come from? Out of what would it be made?

No! It is this 'Consciousness-Peace-I' that takes the shape of the dream and in turn takes the shape of the waking state.

So 'Consciousness-Peace-I' never disappears. It simply takes the shape of every current experience, and when there is no objective experience, it simply remains as it always is.

That is why it is sometimes said that meditation is like being asleep while remaining awake.

It simply means that we remain knowingly as this 'Consciousness-Peace-I,' as that which *is* deep sleep, in the presence of objects – that is, in the waking state. It does not mean that we should act as if we were inert or without feeling.

Every experience of the dream and waking worlds is only this 'Consciousness-Peace-I' taking the shape of thinking, imagining, sensing and perceiving.

That is why Ramana Maharshi said that only that which exists in deep, dreamless sleep is real.

It is *that* which takes the shape of every experience and *that* which is the substance, the Reality, of every experience.

There is only that and, by definition, 'I,' Consciousness, *is* that.

Just This

How is it that there seem to be so many contradictions in expressions of the same teaching, the same understanding?

Some teachings will state the absolute truth over and over again, in various ways, whilst others will appear to condone the separate entity by entertaining ideas in which an apparent person is included.

For instance, one may state, "You have no freedom," and another may state, "You have complete freedom."

If the first statement is addressed to an alleged person, an apparently separate entity, then it is true. If it is addressed to the Presence that we are, the Consciousness that is seeing and understanding these words, it is false.

Conversely if the second statement is addressed to Presence it is true. If to the 'person,' false.

So the words are relative to their context but we should not conclude from this that their meaning is relative. Both answers express the same understanding.

It is the Understanding from which the answer comes, rather than the content of the words themselves, that is important. That Understanding is not something that is known. It is Silence itself.

This Silence is not a blank object. It is not an absence of sound, which in fact is no Silence at all. It is the background of Presence, which is the support and substance of all appearances, including an absence of sound.

It is an alive, open unknowingness that is free to take any shape or any position at any moment, in relation to the moment itself.

The words of the teaching are the shape that this Silence takes and it is this Silence itself that is delivered in the answer.

The words are the packaging. Once the message, this unknowing openness, is delivered, or rather revealed, the packaging can be discarded. The words can be forgotten.

In this way the teaching remains free of fixed formulations, dogma and fundamentalism. It remains fluid, playful, enjoyable, unpredictable and ungraspable. It always leaves us in open unknowingness.

This open unknowingness is what we *are*. It is not something that we *know*.

So, if a question comes from an entrenched belief in the reality of the separate individual, and such a belief usually has its roots in a deep feeling, one answer may just demolish the premise of the question and go straight to the heart of the matter, the belief and feeling of separation, whilst another may take the apparent person by the hand, so to speak, and walk him or her through a process.

It would be simplistic to think that the first answer is necessarily a formulation of the 'direct path,' expressing the highest truth, and the second, a formulation of the 'progressive path,' representing a lesser understanding.

The apparent contradiction between these two positions may not be a contradiction at all. They may both come from the same place and therefore be the same answer.

No formulation of the Reality of experience is completely true. Once we acknowledge this, we relieve words of the impossible burden of trying to express the true nature of experience and, as a result, leave them free to be spoken and heard in playful and creative ways that evoke Reality itself, but never try to frame or grasp it.

A question, by definition, comes from the unknown. The answer comes from the same place.

The only difference between the two is that onto the unknown from which the question comes we superimpose a layer of objectivity and limitation, through seeking and expectation. The answer simply relieves the unknowingness, from which the question comes, of its superimposed limitations.

It returns the veiled unknowingness to an open unknowingness that is silent, empty, free, luminous, transparent and unlimited, ready at any moment to take the shape of… just this…

The Doer

How is Self-knowing brought about?

Are you not present now? Have you not always been present? Have you ever experienced the absence of Consciousness, the cessation of your Existence?

You, Consciousness, are prior to experience. You, Consciousness, are not the result of an experience. All experience is a result of *You*. *You* are not the result of a process.

Therefore your Being, your Reality, and the Peace and Happiness that are inherent therein, cannot be the result of a practice. Any so-called practice that aims for Happiness cannot be called spiritual. It is worldly. It is end-gaining. It is a perpetuation of the strategies of consolation and avoidance that characterise conventional life in the world.

Having said that, such practices also have their place in the revelation of Happiness. And ironically it is precisely because they do not work that they are effective. Their efficiency is in their inefficiency.

Sooner or later this form of worldly practice, this bargaining with God, fails. Our usual strategies of denial last for some time but when all compensations have been exhausted and we have nowhere else to go, a crisis of despair and longing is precipitated.

This unwinding of the tangled knot of seeking is the end of the conventional spiritual search. It is the deep understanding that nothing can be done as an individual, that the individual itself *is* a form of doing.

However, even this last gasp of conventional seeking can be appropriated by the separate self-sense, in an attempt to continue avoiding its own Reality, and with its mantra of, 'There is nothing to do,' it remains imprisoned in the ivory tower of its own isolation.

However, at some point the seeking for Happiness exhausts itself and the unknowing that is laid bare in its absence is revealed as an invitation from another direction, from an unknown direction.

In most cases this invitation will take the form of a teacher. The true teacher is in fact this very Knowingness, and the crisis of despair and longing, whether it comes in one intense afternoon or in a vague feeling of numbness and lack that pervades the years of seeking, is in fact only this Knowingness breaking through into the realm of our everyday experience.

The human teacher is, for most of us, the first form of this Knowingness, and through our association with him or her, in whatever form that may take, we are returned to the Knowingness that is our Self.

In some ways this encounter ends a chapter in our lives. In another way it opens a new one. What we previously thought to be 'practice' or 'doing' is no longer a choice. It is an impossibility. At the same time the offering of the body, the mind and the world to Presence becomes an inevitability.

From the outside this may look like a practice, like something that an individual is doing for a desired end, and it may not differ outwardly from more conventional modes of spiritual seeking. However, it is nothing of the sort. They are worlds apart.

In fact it is not even the offering of the body, the mind and the world. It is the reclaiming of the body, the mind and the world, their re-absorption into that from which they were never for a single moment separated.

This should not really be called practice. It should be called love. In fact, it *is* love.

Many teachings tell us that there is nothing one can do to reach enlightenment.

It would be disingenuous to believe that there is nothing to do, that Consciousness is all there is, that there is no separate entity, simply because we have heard or read it so many times.

Such a belief leaves us worse off than we were in the first place. Not only do we still harbour the original belief in separation and its attendant feelings, but we overlay it with a veneer of 'non-dualism,' embedded in which is the deep belief that the mind only perpetuates ignorance.

If we make the statement that there is nothing that we can do to reach enlightenment, we make it either from understanding, from our own experience, or we make it from hearsay, from belief.

If the statement is made from experience, then it is true.

However, if it is not our experience that there is nothing to do to reach enlightenment, then, by definition, it implies that there is still an apparent personal entity present. That personal entity *is* the apparent doer, feeler, thinker, enjoyer, sufferer, etc.

So if we believe ourselves to be such a doer, it is disingenuous to say that there is nothing to do. It is a contradiction in terms. We are already doing something. To that apparent one it would be more appropriate to say, 'Yes, there is something to be done.'

What is there to be done? Investigate the belief and the feeling as to whether or not what we truly are is a separate entity, an individual doer. When that issue is resolved, the question as to whether or not there is something to be done will not arise.

So the formulation, 'There is nothing to do,' and the formulation, 'There is something to do,' can both be either true or untrue, depending on the understanding from which they are derived. In the end both are irrelevant, but in the beginning both can be helpful.

If we think that either one is truer than the other, then we are stuck at the level of mind. We condone and substantiate mind either through denial or through assertion, and there is not much to choose between those two positions. In fact they are the same position.

However, if we explore the relative truth of *both* statements, we free ourselves from the dogma attached to either position and, in this case, the issue is transcended in Understanding rather than resolved in knowledge.

Origin, Substance And Destiny

Is there a meaning or purpose to life?

Meaning and purpose exist in the mind only.

In deep sleep, for instance, the mind is not present, and no meaning or purpose exists there.

That into which the mind subsides when a question about the nature of experience is answered, *is* its meaning. That is the experience of Understanding.

That into which the body subsides when a desire is fulfilled, *is* its purpose. That is the experience of Happiness or Love.

The experience of Understanding and Happiness is transparent, luminous and Self-knowing.

Transparent in the sense that it is a non-objective experience.

Luminous in the sense that it is present, alive and experienced.

Self-knowing in the sense that it is known, not by any outside agent, but by itself. It is the knowing of itself.

This experience of Understanding and Happiness is the experience of Consciousness knowing itself, knowingly.

That into which the mind and body subside is Consciousness, and Consciousness is present, not just when the mind and body dissolve, but *prior to* and *during* their appearance.

Therefore the true meaning and purpose of life is Consciousness itself, and Consciousness is also its *origin* and *substance.*

It is the origin and substance of all appearances, as well as their destiny.

However, Consciousness is also that into which all appearances dissolve and in that sense it is also their natural fulfilment.

However, it is not the fulfilment or destiny of appearances in the sense that they achieve, become or complete something, because that into which all appearances is resolved is *already* present *before* and *during* the existence of that appearance.

In fact it is already the very substance of every appearance.

Every appearance is, at its origin, already that for which it is destined.

The meaning and purpose of appearances is in their absence.

The meaning and purpose of life is already life itself.

The most extraordinary occurrence ever possible has already taken place. It is already present. There is Consciousness and there is Being.

The tiniest speck of dust ultimately reveals only the presence and identity of Consciousness and Being. What could be more miraculous than that? The most extraordinary miracle would reveal nothing more important than that.

There is only Consciousness, Being.

This is known as 'I,' and also as Happiness, Love, Peace, Beauty and Understanding.

What more meaning and purpose than that could there possibly be?

Love In Search Of Itself

What is the value and function of spiritual seeking?

The purpose of seeking, at the level of the body, is to bring about Happiness and, at the level of the mind, to bring about Understanding.

Inherent in seeking, therefore, is the feeling and the belief that Happiness and Understanding are not already present, and that they can be brought about though the search.

In other words Happiness and Understanding are construed as intermittent states that can be attained at some future time as a result of an activity, and, by implication, that can be lost.

When a desire is fulfilled, Happiness is experienced. When a question is answered, Understanding is revealed.

We presume that it was the fulfilment of the desire that produced the Happiness and the answering of the question that brought about the Understanding.

However, it is the *end* of the desire, not its fulfilment, which reveals the underlying, ever-present Happiness. And it is the *dissolution* of the question rather than its answer that reveals the Understanding that lies behind the mind's activity.

Desire, at the level of the body, and seeking at the level of the mind are, in most cases, forms of agitation. They are modulations of a sense of lack, a sense that something is not right, that something needs to be secured or known.

This agitation is an activity within Consciousness and is an expression of Consciousness. Everything, literally everything, takes place within Consciousness and is an expression of it.

This agitation could be described as the activity whereby Consciousness colours itself in such a way that it seems to obscure itself from itself.

The result is the thought and feeling that something is missing. It is as if Consciousness was saying to itself, 'I am not present. I am not experiencing myself. I do not know myself.'

However, this very thought appears *in* Consciousness and is itself an expression *of* Consciousness.

That 'something' that is supposed to be missing is Consciousness itself.

The 'I' that is experiencing the feeling, 'I am not experiencing myself,' and the 'I' that is thinking the thought, 'I do not know myself,' is *already* that One that seems not to be experienced or known.

Although Consciousness is in fact always, only, ever experiencing itself, it veils itself from itself and therefore feels that it is not present.

In fact Consciousness is still only experiencing itself, even during the appearance of the feeling that something is missing.

That very feeling is itself still the experience of Consciousness knowing itself.

However, Consciousness does not know this, so to speak. It disguises itself. It veils itself and hence the search for itself begins.

Consciousness forgets that it is always experiencing itself and projects a state called Happiness that can be found as a result of an activity in the body, and a state called Understanding that can be found as a result of an activity in the mind.

Happiness and Understanding are construed as something other than Consciousness, something that has objective qualities, something that is not always present, something that can be sought and found.

However, the Happiness and the Understanding that are desired and sought are themselves simply the experience of Consciousness knowing itself knowingly. That is what Happiness and Understanding are.

The agitation called 'seeking' *veils* the inherent Happiness and Understanding. It does not produce it.

When Consciousness veils or forgets itself, it conceives of itself as an experience of Happiness in the body and/or an experience of Understanding in the mind. It then sets about searching for them both.

However, Happiness is not an experience in the body and Understanding is not an experience in the mind.

Happiness is another name for Consciousness. It is the particular name Consciousness gives itself when it experiences itself at the end of a desire.

Likewise Understanding is another name for Consciousness. It is the particular name Consciousness gives itself when it experiences itself at the end of a thought.

Both Happiness and Understanding are already present, as Consciousness itself, *prior* to seeking, rather than as a result of it.

Seeking itself is simply the name and the shape that Consciousness takes as it sets out in search of itself.

And Happiness and Understanding are the experience of Consciousness recognising itself at the end of that search.

Consciousness never goes anywhere or becomes anything other than itself, even during the apparent process of forgetting, searching and finding.

Presence is never lost and never found. It is ever-present.

The activities of forgetting, searching and finding are all equally modes of its own Being, in which it is always, only experiencing itself in changing names and forms.

We invest an object with the capacity to produce Happiness or Peace and then pursue it. Once the desired object is obtained we briefly feel Happiness and mistakenly suppose that it was the object that gave rise to it.

However, it was the acquisition of the object that led to the *end* of the desire, not to the *fulfilment* of the desire. The true desire was for Happiness, not for the object. The object leads to the end of the desire, not to Happiness.

However, the end of the desire *is* the end of the mind's agitation. This agitation is nothing other than Consciousness thinking and feeling that the Happiness and Peace that are inherent in itself are not present and, as a result, searching for them 'elsewhere.'

The cessation of the agitation is the end of the search.

Consciousness no longer projects the thought and feeling, 'I am not present and therefore need to find myself somewhere else.' It withdraws this projection and as a result experiences itself as it is, tastes itself, has a glimpse of itself.

With the withdrawal of this projection, our longing is taken back to its source.

Happiness and Peace are already present in the longing but they are veiled by its seeking for an object. As soon as longing is relieved of its objectivity it is revealed as Happiness and Peace itself.

Of course Consciousness is always, only, ever itself. It never leaves itself. Where could it go? It had just veiled itself with desire, with the thought and feeling, 'I need something else in order to be happy.'

Happiness is not an experience that Consciousness *has*. It is what Consciousness *is*. That is why Joy is said to be causeless.

Consciousness experiences itself as this Happiness or Peace every time it stops escaping from itself through desire (or fear). It is for this reason that the desire for Happiness is universal. It is inherent in the Consciousness that *is* each one of us.

Happiness is the taste of Consciousness knowing itself, knowingly.

Once we see clearly that it is the *ending* of desire, rather than its fulfilment, that reveals the inherent Happiness, we no longer *search* for an object to make us happy. We may desire an object with which to *express* Happiness, but this Happiness is not dependent on the object.

Happiness cannot have a cause. Only unhappiness can have a cause. In fact, unhappiness always has a cause and that cause is always an object. Even the term 'unhappiness' contains within it the knowledge that unhappiness is somehow the veiling of Happiness, that Happiness is contained within it. However, we never describe Happiness as 'unmisery.'

Happiness is not the opposite of unhappiness. It is present behind and within all the happy and unhappy states of the mind and the body.

Happiness is not relative. It does not come and go, any more than the sky comes and goes. The fact that it seems to appear and disappear is obviously true on the relative level, just as the sky seems to appear and disappear. However, that does not make it absolutely true.

Happiness, like Beauty and Love, is absolute, not relative. They are all inherent in Consciousness, and as such they do not change or disappear. They are the experience of Consciousness knowing itself, knowingly.

When the mind dissolves at the end of a thought, Consciousness recognises itself, and this recognition is called Understanding.

When the body dissolves at the end of a bodily sensation, Consciousness recognises itself, and this recognition is called Happiness or Love.

When the world dissolves at the end of a perception, Consciousness recognises itself, and this recognition is called Beauty.

The words Understanding, Happiness, Love and Beauty are all synonyms for Consciousness, for 'I.' They do not refer to objects.

Peace is beyond the mind, Joy is uncaused, Beauty has no form, Love is unconditional and Understanding knows no object.

There is Peace, Joy, Beauty, Love and Understanding and these are all experiences of the transparent, luminous, empty, Knowingness of Presence.

They are all one thing that has or knows no opposite. They are unconditional.

All unhappy states are only this Consciousness forgetting itself.

They are simply the names we give to Consciousness when it fails to recognise itself, or rather for the belief and feeling that Consciousness entertains, that it is not already, directly knowing itself.

They are imaginary as states, but real as Consciousness.

Everything ultimately comes from this unconditional Love.

Openness Sensitivity Vulnerability And Availability

If I'm honest I want to get rid of my suffering.

The ultimate cause of suffering* is ignorance of our true nature, that is – the *ignoring* of our true nature, the ignoring of Consciousness.

We take that which is unreal to be real and that which is real to be unreal.

All objective experience – that is the mind, body and world – is made out of thinking and imagining, sensing, and seeing, hearing, touching, tasting and smelling.

What happens to our entire objective experience, including all of our suffering, when all of these are removed? It vanishes.

Where is suffering in deep sleep? It is non-existent.

And if we go deeply into our experience at any given moment, we find that suffering is also non-existent there. In fact deep sleep and the present moment share much in common, whilst the past and the future have much in common with the dream state.

Suffering, by definition, requires the presence of a separate entity for its existence. However, that separate entity is itself non-existent, imaginary. What can we say therefore of this separate entity's suffering? It is no more real than the entity around which it revolves, although of course it is a powerful illusion.

If we go deeply into the experience of suffering while it is actually taking place, we find that the one around whom the suffering revolves is not present. It is present as a thought or a sensation, but the entity itself is not present.

---

*It is psychological suffering, not physical pain, that is referred to here.

To return to objective experience, what is thinking, imagining, sensing, seeing, hearing, touching, tasting and smelling, made of? It is made of knowing or experiencing.

And what would happen, if knowing or experiencing were removed from them? They would vanish.

Knowing or experiencing is the ingredient which is common to them all, and without which none of them exist.

Thinking, imagining, sensing, seeing, hearing, touching, tasting and smelling are the particular forms that knowing or experiencing take.

And what is knowing or experiencing made of?

It is made of that which is conscious, that which knows and experiences. That is, it is made of Consciousness, and this Consciousness is our most intimate Self.

What happens if we try to remove Consciousness? We cannot. We cannot go further back in our experience than Consciousness.

If we have followed this line of reasoning, not just intellectually but in our actual experience, we have by the same token, whether we realise it or not, acknowledged that the real substance of every objective experience is Consciousness itself.

We have acknowledged that the known is made of knowing and that knowing is made of Consciousness.

You, I, We, Consciousness is the Reality of all things. That is our moment by moment experience. It is our lived, intimate, direct experience, not simply an intellectual idea.

That which *seems* to be real in every experience is a ripple within the ocean of our Self. It is made out of mind-stuff, thinking, sensing and perceiving, and it vanishes in the same way that the mind-stuff out of which a dream is made, vanishes.

However, the *substance* of that mind-stuff is our Self, Consciousness. It seems to be unreal and non-existent from the point of view of objective experience, but in fact it turns out to be the very essence, the Reality of that experience.

The only problem is that we take that which is unreal to be real and that which is real to be unreal.

And even that is not a problem, because that very appearance itself, that apparent problem, is itself made out of the ever-present, unchanging Reality of our Self, Consciousness.

I understand that in theory, but...

Theoretical understanding is only possible in relation to an object. That is because, when we think of an object, the mind forms an image or a concept of that object, but never actually comes in contact with the object itself.

The mind forms a representation of the apparent object in the terms of its own code – that is, in images and concepts.

However, the thought about Consciousness is different. The mind cannot represent that which has no objective qualities, so when it goes towards Consciousness, it collapses. It just cannot go there.

How could a three-dimensional object enter a two-dimensional plane? How could a two-dimensional plane enter a one-dimensional point? And how could the one-dimensional object of mind enter the zero-dimensional space of Consciousness?

This collapse of the mind as it tries to 'see' or 'understand' Consciousness reveals the ever-present Consciousness that was veiled by the very activity of seeking.

This does not deny the validity of seeking. On the contrary, it validates it!

The value of seeking is that as long as it is taken all the way back to its Source, it brings itself to its own limit and dissolves there. That into which it dissolves is that for which it was seeking.

Thinking cannot get rid of thinking, but it can go to the limit of thinking. Seeking cannot get rid of seeking, but it can go to the end of seeking.

If seeking is not denied or frustrated, if it is allowed to run its full course, it will come to its natural limit. However, it is Consciousness that dissolves the seeking thought, just as water dissolves the sugar cube.

Seeking should be allowed to run its course for it is in the *dissolution* of thinking, not in the *frustration* of thinking, that Consciousness is revealed, that Consciousness tastes itself.

Seeking never finds what it is looking for. It is dissolved in it.

From the mind's point of view, it is the end of seeking, rather than its fulfilment, that brings about the revelation of Presence.

From the point of view of Reality, it is the experience of Consciousness recognising itself, that brings about the end of seeking.

However, this should not be taken as an incentive to stop seeking. On the contrary, it can be taken as an indication that seeking should run its full course, should fully explore its own limits.

Only then will the mind come to an end naturally in Understand-ing. This Understanding is itself the experience of Consciousness knowing itself knowingly.

This is a very different situation from one in which the mind is frustrated as a result of having its validity denied, or whose natural inquisitiveness is disciplined through effort. Such a mind is never truly brought to an end. It is not peaceful. It is suppressed.

Such a mind simply forms a belief and, in doing so, it perpetuates itself. It rests on that belief, falls asleep on it, anaesthetises itself, fooling itself into thinking that it has come to an end. This is not Understanding. It is inertia.

The process of exploring the nature of experience is the process through which the mind is truly brought to its limit.

The mind does not *find* Understanding. It *dies* in it.

But how is this non-objective Understanding applied to our very real objective lives?

We don't try to apply it. We simply let this Understanding express itself naturally in our life.

Have we been *applying* ignorance to our life all these years? No! We just mistook appearances for Reality, and that attitude, of its own accord, conditioned our subsequent experience very efficiently, without our having to make a special effort to apply it.

We do not need to *apply* ignorance to our lives to make it effective. It works very nicely by itself!

Similarly Understanding.

If we have understood, in our own way, what has been said here, we just allow that Understanding to express itself naturally. It will condition our life in just the same way that our previous understanding conditioned our life effortlessly.

When we go into a darkened room, we see nothing to begin with. Slowly shapes start to emerge until in the end we see quite clearly. We do not have to do anything to facilitate this. It happens naturally.

Likewise here. Understanding, which is not a knowing of *something*, but rather *Knowingness* itself, permeates every aspect of our life from an unknown direction. It just happens naturally.

On the outside there may or may not be much change. That is not important. But on the inside there is more and more Peace, Freedom, Happiness and Love.

Old habits still come up, but as they are no longer fuelled by mistaken ideas, they show up less and less frequently.

This change happens either gradually or rapidly. It doesn't matter. Who is the one that cares? That one is non-existent. Perhaps some of these habits may stay around forever. So what? We all have characters that are conditioned at the level of the body and mind.

Advaita, Non-Duality, is not a bland whitewash of all the individual elements in each of our characters. In fact it is rather the opposite.

Individuality means un-divided. Individuality is the unique expression of the undivided whole, which each body/mind expresses, and it tends to flourish rather than diminish, when we are relieved of the strait-jacket of ignorance – that is, when we stop ignoring our Self.

Similarly, Non-Duality is not an immunisation against feeling. In fact it is the opposite. It is complete openness, sensitivity, vulnerability and availability.

Actually, suffering is our *resistance* to feeling, rather than a feeling itself.

So we don't try to *use* this Understanding. We allow it to use us. We allow it to shape our life. We don't put it into another strait-jacket and dictate how it should operate.

Consciousness is absolute Freedom. We allow this Freedom to express itself as it will, how it will, where it will and when it will.

In one body/mind this might take the shape of a character that is quiet and sensitive, whilst in another it may express itself in a wild and exuberant way.

We should not be misled by appearances. It is the attitude of inner freedom that is the hallmark of Understanding, and this attitude of inner freedom uses all possible means of expression and communication.

What part do feelings and the body have to play in this investigation?

Much of the mind's activity is designed to avoid feeling. For instance, any form of repetitive, compulsive thinking is usually a sign that just below its surface lies an uncomfortable well of feelings.

However, sooner or later, these uncomfortable feelings begin to percolate through the strategies and coping mechanisms that the mind has constructed.

The first impulse is usually to escape them through thinking and activity. In this way the cycle of seeking is generated over and over again.

However, each time seeking is brought to an end in Understanding, one of the mind's avenues of escape is cut off.

As a result, when uncomfortable feelings resurface, we find that there are fewer and fewer possibilities of denial and avoidance.

We no longer escape these feelings. We have the courage to face them. We do not do anything with them or to them and, by the same token, we do not deny, avoid or suppress them.

The impulse to escape them through thinking stills appears, but that impulse itself is seen to be just one more uncomfortable feeling.

Sooner or later a deep conviction appears, a conviction that these feelings cannot be escaped, avoided, manipulated or glossed over. Nor need they be. And with this conviction comes the courage to face them.

We just allow them to be.

The openness, sensitivity, vulnerability and availability that Consciousness is, that we are, *is* the allowing of all things.

This courage and openness to face our feelings is an invitation for deeper and deeper layers of feeling to emerge.

It is for this reason that, to begin with, the spiritual path does not always appear to be peaceful. Often there is an apparent increase in the level of discomfort and agitation.

However, that is a misinterpretation of what is really occurring. It is not *new* layers of discomfort and dis-ease that are being generated. It is age-old habits of feeling that are being exposed.

To begin with it is these feelings that occupy our attention. They seem to be all-consuming. However, as there is less and less impulse to avoid them, the welcoming space in which they are allowed to be, without any agenda for or against, is noticed more and more.

The welcoming space of our own Awareness, which once seemed to be in the background or even eclipsed by these all-consuming feelings, begins to emerge and, as a result, the feelings begin to recede.

In fact, they don't really recede. Devoid of the mental commentary that previously gave them meaning and validity, they are experienced more and more as innocuous bodily sensations.

In this way they lose their bite. They are neutralised, not because we have done anything to them, but simply because they have been seen for what they are.

Even to say that they are bodily sensations is too much. If we explore them in the same way that we explore any other object, we find that their very substance *is* the substance of the welcoming Presence in which they appear.

They have no separating power. There is no suffering in them.

These sensations are like drops of milk in a jar of water. They are currents rippling through the ocean of our Self.

Time and Memory

It is often said that time is an illusion, but if I look back at my life, memories seem to validate the existence of time?

Memory seems to validate time, but if we look at it closely we see that it in fact validates the timeless, changelessness of Consciousness.

Memory creates the appearance of time, in which objects are considered to exist independently from one another, and through which they are considered to evolve.

However, we have no experience of a past that stretches out indefinitely behind the 'present moment.' And we have no experience of a 'present moment' rolling forever forward into the future.

The idea that time is like a container, that houses all the events of our lives is in fact a temporal representation of Consciousness, in the mind.

And likewise, the idea that space is like a container, that houses all the objects in the world is a spatial representation of Consciousness, in the mind.

Events do not appear in time and objects do not appear in space. They both appear in Consciousness.

When an object, which is simply an appearance in Consciousness, is present, its subsequent recollection is obviously not yet present. It is non-existent. And likewise when the recollection, which is simply a thought in Consciousness, takes place, the original object is no longer present. It is non-existent.

In other words, two objects cannot appear in Consciousness at the same time. When one is present the other is not, and vice versa.

How then can a non-existent object be remembered? It cannot. An object is never remembered.

It is in fact a third thought which apparently connects the second thought, the recollection, with the first thought, the object. And when that third thought is present, neither the object nor its recollection are present. This third thought is therefore a concept that does not relate to an experience.

Time and memory are apparently created with that third thought, but have no existence apart from that thought.

At the same time we have a deep conviction that the experience of the first object is somehow still present in the form of a memory, that the experience was not entirely lost. Yes! That which was truly present then is truly present now. Consciousness! The object borrows its apparent Reality, its apparent continuity, from Consciousness.

Nothing is ever lost. That which took the shape of the object then, is taking the shape of its 'recollection' now.

However, the idea of 'then' collapses with this understanding, and with it the idea of 'now,' because these two ideas depend on one another.

Therefore time and memory as such are never experienced. The apparent continuity of an object, which memory seems to validate, is in fact the continuity of Consciousness.

It is the ever-present Now.

The spinning wheel that appears on a computer screen when a function is taking place appears to be composed of a dot that circles round and round.

In fact, it is composed of numerous individual dots, each one appearing and disappearing in rapid succession.

In this way the illusion of a single dot travelling round and round is created and, even when we know this is the case, the illusion is still very convincing.

The appearance of a single dot is created by numerous intermittent appearances. The dots have no relation to each other. They are only related to the screen, to the background.

The only thing they have in common is the background of the screen. It is the screen, which is behind and within the dots, that is illumined when each dot appears.

It is the *permanence* of the screen that is indicated by the *apparent* continuity of the travelling dot. There is in fact no travelling dot.

Similarly continuity in time is in fact the ever-presence of Consciousness.

It is the ever-present background of Consciousness, rather than the continuity of time, that is indicated by memory and which itself gives apparent continuity to appearances.

The separate self is one such dot, given apparent continuity by the presence of Consciousness. As Einstein said, "The separate self is an optical delusion in Consciousness."

The continuity with which the sense of 'I' shines is the Ever-Presentness of Presence.

However, we mistakenly attribute this Ever-Presentness to an object, to the body/mind.

In the Christian tradition, this mistake is referred to as the 'original sin'. It is the original mistake, as a result of which the story of a separate entity that exists in time is born. All psychological suffering depends on this original mistake.

Timeless Presence seems to become an object that is present in time.

Ever-Presence seems to become continuity in time and permanence in space.

The Eternal Now shrinks itself into an endless expanse of time and space.

However, even as it does this, this Eternal Now never ceases being what it is.

How is it possible to have an objectless experience?

It is difficult to answer this question as the question itself contains an implicit assumption that we experience objects. Of course there is the appearance of objects. However, experience is in fact always objectless.

Instead of starting with objects, for which we have no experiential evidence, and trying to go back to Consciousness from there, start instead with Consciousness, which is an absolute fact of experience, and try to go from there to objects. It is not possible!

So we simply stay with the facts of our experience and allow our deep-seated convictions and certainties about the nature of experience to be unravelled in this disinterested contemplation. The world, as a result, returns to its proper place.

Does 'Consciousness experiencing itself' mean, in ordinary terms, that that is a non-experience? If so, what does it mean to have 'experiencing' when there is no experience?

The presumption is that experience implies objects and that when there are no objects there is no experience. As an acknowledgement of this, the word 'experience' is used to describe what is normally conceived of as 'experience with objects' and 'non-objective experience' to indicate experience without objects.

Again we cannot really resolve this issue whilst there is the conviction that objects exist as an actual experience. From our ordinary point of view objects slowly disappear as we fall asleep until, in deep sleep, no objects at all are experienced. We therefore normally conceive of deep sleep as a state in which there is no experience.

However, even if for the time being, we provisionally grant the existence of objects, the essential ingredient of every experience is Consciousness itself. This is easy to check for ourselves by asking what would happen to experiencing if an object, such as this book, were now to be removed. Nothing! It would continue, although it would have a slightly different character. However, what would happen to experiencing if Consciousness were to be removed? It would vanish absolutely.

So the experiencing part of an object belongs to Consciousness, not to the object, if such an object exists. So in deep sleep, when Consciousness is, so to speak, all alone, with no objective content, the Experiencingness of Consciousness remains exactly as it always is, pure experiencing.

So the experiencing that is present during the apparent existence of objects is no different from the experiencing that is present during the absence of objects. It is only referred to as objective experience and non-objective experience, respectively, as a concession to the mind that conceives the existence of separate, independent objects.

Consciousness is Experiencingness and because Consciousness is always present, so experiencing is always present. How could this Experiencingness not be experiencing itself all the time?

The Moon's Light

Consciousness is present even in thoughts and feelings that do not appear to express the true nature of our experience, such as, 'I am the mind,' or, 'I am the body.'

The sense of identity that pervades these thoughts and feelings, the 'I am' part, *is* the presence of Consciousness. It is only the inadvertent association of this 'I am' with a body and a mind that results in the belief and feeling that we are separate, limited entities.

Consciousness is the most intimate thing we know. The intimacy that we seek and love in relationships is precisely this intimacy of our own Self.

Consciousness shines as the sense of 'I,' irrespective of what it is identified with.

The fact that Consciousness *seems* to be limited to a mind or a body does not mean that it *is* limited. It means that we *seem* to experience it as such. It seems to experience itself as such.

We, Consciousness, seem to experience our Self as limited, and we enjoy and suffer the inevitable consequences of this apparent limitation. However, Consciousness is not actually limited by this or any other thought or feeling.

Even if it appears that the moon shines with its own light, this appearance does not change the fact that it is the sun's light with which it shines.

In every appearance of the world, Existence is present, independent of the particular character of the appearance.

The *Existence* of every object *is* the presence of Being, in just the same way that the sense of *identity* in any thought or feeling about ourselves *is* the presence of Consciousness.

Consciousness is to myself what Existence or Being is to the world.

The sense of 'I' in any thought or feeling is not just conscious. It is present. It is Being as well as Consciousness.

'I' is Consciousness. 'Am' is Being. The experience of 'I am' is the most intimate and familiar experience we know. It is the experience of the oneness of Consciousness and Being.

When this Oneness divides itself into a body and a world, it veils itself from itself.

Likewise every object appears within Consciousness and its Existence cannot be separated from the presence of Consciousness.

Therefore in the experience of any object we also experience the oneness of Consciousness and Being.

So whether we start from ourselves or from the world, we are brought back to the oneness of Consciousness and Being.

The mystic tends to start with the investigation into the nature of the Self. The artist tends to start with the investigation into the world. But both ultimately arrive at the same conclusion, that Consciousness is the fundamental Reality of the world, that Consciousness and Being are one.

The Natural Condition

Consciousness is naturally one with all things. It is one with the totality of experience.

However, at times, Consciousness contracts itself, shrinks itself into a body and this self-contraction requires constant maintenance.

Left without maintenance, the self-contraction gradually unwinds and Consciousness returns to its natural condition.

Desiring and fearing are two of the main ways that Consciousness maintains its self-contraction as an apparent separate entity.

As soon as a desire is fulfilled it comes to an end. The end of the desire is the end of the maintenance of the self-contraction and, as a result, Consciousness returns to itself – that is, it experiences again its own unlimited nature. This experience is called Happiness.

Consciousness does not in fact return to itself. It just recognises itself. It knows itself again as this unlimited openness, welcoming, sensitivity. It no longer pretends to be other. It no longer hides itself from itself.

Consciousness has become so accustomed to shrinking itself into the frame of a body and a mind that the release from this self-contraction is often accompanied by a sense of elation or expansion.

However, as Consciousness becomes more and more accustomed to abiding in and as itself, as it no longer pretends to be a separate entity and to go out of itself in search of itself, this natural abidance in and as itself becomes normal and ordinary.

In fact, it is the self-contraction, that once seemed to be so normal and ordinary, that now becomes extraordinary.

Blasphemy is the claim that, 'I am God.' However, the separate entity is entirely non-existent, so there is no question of it being God or anything else for that matter.

The real blasphemy is to think, 'I am a separate entity.' With that thought Consciousness denies its own unlimited, universal sovereignty. It surrenders its Freedom. It is its freedom to do so!

Out of this Freedom, Consciousness projects the mind, the body and the world through the faculties of thinking, imagining, sensing and perceiving.

In the natural condition, this projection is known and felt to be taking place within Consciousness and every part of it is known and felt equally as an expression of Consciousness, *as* Consciousness itself.

However, at times Consciousness divides the totality of experience into two camps. Everything that is part of the 'not me' camp is called 'the world.' Everything that is part of the 'me' camp is called 'the body/mind.'

It is with the thought and feeling 'I am *not* this,' that Consciousness projects the world *outside* itself. And it is with the thought and the feeling, 'I *am* this,' that Consciousness simultaneously identifies itself with, and thereby limits itself to, a body/mind.

This cycle of projecting the mind, body and world every morning and withdrawing the projection every night, as well as many other times during the day, continues in exactly the same way even when Consciousness has come to recognise its own unlimited Freedom.

What ceases is Consciousness' habit of identifying itself with *one* part of the projection and separating itself from *another.* The thought and feeling, 'I am *this* part of my projection, but not *that* part,' 'I am the body but I am not the world,' ceases.

It may continue to project an image of a separate entity with its own life story, from time to time, but it no longer limits itself to this projection.

Even if it reappears from time to time, it is quickly recognised as an old habit that is not substantiated by actual experience and it is abandoned.

There is nothing wrong with the projection of a separate entity. It is essential for many aspects of life. It is only the exclusive identification with it that is problematic.

As Consciousness sees clearly that the entire spectrum of this projection takes place *within* itself, it no longer separates it into 'me' and 'other.'

It sees all things in and as itself.

If you would like to enquire about anything that is written in this book, please contact the author through the non-duality section of his website, www.rupertspira.com

Related Titles from Non-Duality Press

Eternity Now; Francis Lucille
I Am; Jean Klein
Be Who You Are; Jean Klein
Who Am I? Jean Klein
Beyond Knowledge; Jean Klein
Living Truth; Jean Klein

For these and other titles from Non-Duality Press please visit:
www.non-dualitybooks.com

CONSCIOUS.TV

CONSCIOUS.TV is a new TV channel broadcasting through the internet (www.conscious.tv); it will soon be available as a micro-channel on satellite via Sky in the UK. The channel aims to stimulate debate, question, enquire, inform, enlighten, encourage and inspire people in the areas of Consciousness, Health and Psychology.

There are already interviews online with communicators of Non-Duality, including two with Rupert Spira, and other authors whose books are published by Non-Duality Press.

Do check out the station as we would welcome your feedback. We are also interested in suggestions for other people that you would like to see interviewed on Conscious.tv..

Email us at info@conscious.tv with your ideas or if you would like to be on our email newsletter list.

Printed in the United Kingdom by
Lightning Source UK Ltd., Milton Keynes
137014UK00003B/11/P